Business
Calculations

Also from Stanley Thornes (Publishers) Ltd.

A Greer NEW COMPREHENSIVE MATHEMATICS FOR O-LEVEL
A Greer C.S.E. MATHEMATICS–The Core Course
A Greer C.S.E. MATHEMATICS–The Special Topics
A Greer A FIRST COURSE IN STATISTICS
Greer and Hancox TABLES, DATA AND FORMULAE FOR MATHEMATICIANS
R Etheridge, A Greer and K Arnold NUMERACY AND ACCOUNTING
A Greer REVISION PRACTICE IN ARITHMETIC
A Greer REVISION PRACTICE IN ALGEBRA
A Greer REVISION PRACTICE IN GEOMETRY AND TRIGONOMETRY
A Greer REVISION PRACTICE IN NEW MATHEMATICS
A Greer REVISION PRACTICE IN STATISTICS
C M Cox PRACTICE PAPERS IN MATHEMATICS–Book 1 and Book 2

a full list of titles is available on request from the publisher

Business Calculations
for BEC and Other First Courses

A Greer
Formerly Senior Lecturer, Gloucestershire College of Arts and Technology

Stanley Thornes (Publishers) Ltd.

© A Greer 1978   Diagrams © Stanley Thornes (Publishers) Ltd., 1978

All rights reserved. No part of this publication may be reproduced, stored in a retrieval system, or transmitted in any form or by any means, electronic, mechanical, photocopying, recording or otherwise, without the prior written consent of the copyright holder.

First published in 1978 by Stanley Thornes (Publishers) Ltd.,
Educa House, Old Station Drive, off Leckhampton Road, CHELTENHAM GL53 0DN

ISBN 0 85950 480 8
Reprinted 1982
Reprinted 1983 with minor amendments

Typeset by Avontype, Bristol

Printed and bound in Great Britain by
The Pitman Press, Bath

Preface

This book covers all the objectives laid down in the Business Education Council syllabus for its General Award in the Module of Business Calculations (Module 2). The aim has been to provide basic numeracy using examples from various business activities. Much of the material has been taken from my Arithmetic for Commerce (published 1976) but further text has been added where necessary.

A large number of graded exercises have been provided in each chapter and the student should find it possible to work from relatively easy problems to a situation in which confidence in dealing with harder problems is acquired.

At the end of each chapter there is a summary which gives details of all the important points raised in the chapter. There is also, at the end of most chapters, a Mental Test and a Self-Test. The Mental Test consists of basically simple problems which can each be solved in a few seconds but which, nevertheless, bring out the important points given in the chapter summary. The Self-Tests consist, in the main, of objective type questions. Such tests are growing in popularity with examiners and they give the student a chance to assess his or her progress.

In addition, at the end of the book there is a set of Revision Exercises. All the questions in this set are of the type found in examinations at this level. The idea is that the student is given the opportunity of answering examination type questions and gaining experience in examination technique.

A. Greer   *Gloucester*, 1978

Contents

Chapter 1   Operations in Arithmetic   1
Some definitions — addition — subtraction — arithmetical signs, terms and symbols — multiplication — long multiplication — checking the accuracy of a multiplication — division — short division — long division — tests for divisibility — sequence of arithmetical operations.

Chapter 2   Fractions   12
Vulgar fractions — reducing a fraction to its lowest terms — types of fractions — lowest common multiple — lowest common denominator — addition of fractions — subtraction of fractions — combined addition and subtraction — multiplication — cancelling — division of fractions — operations with fractions.

Chapter 3   The Decimal System   24
Addition and subtraction of decimals — multiplication and division of decimals — long multiplication — long division — significant figures — rough checks for calculations — fraction to decimal conversion — conversion of decimals to fractions.

Chapter 4   Money and Simple Accounts   35
The British system — addition and subtraction — balancing — financial statements — petty cash book — multiplication and division — invoices.

Chapter 5   The Metric System   45
The metric system for length — the metric system for mass — the addition and subtraction of metric quantities — multiplying and dividing metric quantities — domestic problems.

Chapter 6   Areas   53
Unit of length — units of area — area of a rectangle — the square — the parallelogram — area of a triangle — area of a trapezium — mensuration of a circle — area of a circle

Chapter 7   The Imperial System of Units   62
The imperial system for length — the imperial system for mass — the imperial system for capacity — conversion from imperial units into metric units — areas of rectilinear figures — units of area.

Chapter 8   Electronic Calculators   66
Limiting the answer to a reasonable number of significant figures — rough checks and feasibility of an answer — rearranging a problem to ease calculation — overflow — calculating powers of numbers.

Chapter 9 **Percentages** **71**

Converting fractions to percentages — converting decimals to percentages — percentage of a quantity — percentage profit and loss — mark up — margin — relation between margin and mark up — gross and net profits — discount — trade discount — invoices with discount.

Chapter 10 **Statistics** **85**

Statistical averages — charts and graphs — axes of reference — scales — coordinates — drawing a graph — the pie chart — the proportionate bar chart — the horizontal bar chart — the vertical bar chart — representing information on pictograms — interpreting charts and diagrams.

Revision Questions **106**

Answers **109**

Index **115**

1. Operations in Arithmetic

UNDERSTAND THE FOUR BASIC RULES OF ARITHMETIC
Perform both written and mental calculations involving addition, subtraction, multiplication and division of integers.

Introduction

In this chapter the basic operations of arithmetic are revised. We will add, subtract, multiply and divide numbers. Since arithmetic is all about numbers let us first consider what numbers are and how they are represented.

Some Definitions

Numbers are represented by symbols which are called *digits*. There are nine digits which are 1, 2, 3, 4, 5, 6, 7, 8 and 9. We also use the symbol 0 (i.e. zero) where no digit exists. Digits and zero may be combined to represent any number.

Numeration expresses numbers in words — zero, one, two, three, four, five, six, seven, eight and nine.

Notation expresses numbers in figures or symbols (0, 1, 2, 3, 4, 5, 6, 7, 8, 9). These are all unit figures. The next number, ten, is 10 which is a combination of one and zero. 11 (eleven) is the combination of one and one and it equals ten plus one. 20 (twenty) is the combination of two and zero and it equals two tens. Ten tens are one hundred and ten hundreds are one thousand and so on.

   100   indicates one hundred
   900   indicates nine hundreds
   954   indicates nine hundreds, five tens and four units
  1000   indicates one thousand
  8000   indicates eight thousands
  9999   indicates nine thousands, nine hundreds, nine tens and nine units

Note that in the case of the number 9999:

  9 9 9 9
  d c b a

	a is a units figure and equals	9
b	is a tens figure and equals	9 0
c	is a hundreds figure and equals	9 0 0
d	is a thousands figure and equals	9 0 0 0

In arithmetic the sign + means plus or add and the sign = means equals. Thus,

$$7+2=9$$

The number $9999 = 9000+900+90+9$

If we want to write six hundreds, five tens and seven units then we write 657. If we want to write four hundred and seven units we write 407; the zero keeps the place for the missing tens.

eight thousand and thirty five is written 8035
eight thousand and nine is written 8009
ten thousand is written 10 000
one hundred thousand is written 100 000
one thousand thousand is called one million which is written 1 000 000.
8 000 000 indicates eight million
37 895 762 indicates thirty seven million, eight hundred and ninety five thousand, seven hundred and sixty two.

In the number 37 895 762 we have grouped the digits in threes with a space between them. This space takes the place of the comma which was traditionally used to group the figures of a number into threes. The change has taken place because many foreign countries use a comma instead of a decimal point.

Exercise 1

Write the following in figures:

1) four hundred and fifty seven
2) nine thousand, five hundred and thirty six
3) seven thousand, seven hundred and seventy seven
4) three thousand and eight
5) seven hundred and five
6) thirty thousand and twenty eight
7) five thousand and ninety
8) four thousand nine hundred and four
9) one hundred and twenty five thousand, nine hundred and six
10) three million, eight hundred thousand and seven
11) ninety five million, eight hundred and twenty seven thousand
12) three hundred million and nine

Write the following numbers in words:

13) 225
14) 8321
15) 3017
16) 3960
17) 1807
18) 20 004
19) 17 000
20) 198 376
21) 200 005
22) 7 365 231
23) 27 000 309

Addition

When adding numbers together place the figures in columns making sure that all the units figures are placed under one another, that all the tens figures are placed beneath each other and so on. Thus all the figures having the same place value fall in the same column.

OPERATIONS IN ARITHMETIC

Example 1 Add together 4219, 583, 98 and 1287.

4219	Start off by adding the units column. Thus 7 and 8 make 15 and 3 makes 18 and 9 makes 27. Place the 7 in the units column of the answer and carry the 2 forward to the tens column. Adding this we have 2 and 8 is 10 and 9 is 19 and 8 is 27 and 1 is 28. Place the 8 in the tens column of the answer and carry the 2 forward to the hundreds column which we now add. 2 and 2 is 4 and 5 is 9 and 2 is 11. We write a 1 in the hundreds column of the answer and carry 1 forward to the thousands column which we now add. 1 and 1 is 2 and 4 is 6. Writing the 6 in the thousands column of the answer we see that the answer to the addition is 6187.
583	
98	
1287	
6187	

Example 2 Find the value of $17\,638+108\,749+1011+2\,345\,008$.

The $+$ sign simply means add the numbers together and our problem is to add the four numbers. As before we write them in a column so that digits having the same place values are written beneath each other.

17 638	Add up the units column from bottom to top, saying audibly, 9, 18, 26. Write 6 in the units column of the answer and carry the 2 forward to the tens column. Add the tens column as 2, 3, 7 and 10. Write 0 in the tens column of the answer and carry the 1 forward to the hundreds column. Carry on in this way with the remaining columns until the answer is obtained.
108 749	
1 011	
2 345 008	
2 472 406	

Exercise 2

Find the values of each of the following:

1) $96+247+8$
2) $109+57+3478+926$
3) $35\,068+21\,007+905+1178+32$
4) $23\,589+7\,987\,432+234\,068+9871+324\,689$
5) $15\,437+1344+1626+107\,924$

Subtraction

Subtraction means taking away. Let us take 5 from 6. We know that 1 is left. We write $6-5=1$ which we read as six minus five equals 1.

Example 3 Subtract 17 from 59.

59	Place 17 under 59. 7 from 9 leaves 2. Write 2 in the units column of the answer and then 1 from 5 leaves 4. Writing 4 in the tens column of the answer we see that $59-17=42$.
17	
42	

There are two methods by which subtraction can be performed. Consider
$$15 - 8 = 7$$
1st method: Take 8 from 15. We have 7 left.

2nd method: If to 7 we add 8 then we obtain 15. 7 is therefore the difference between 15 and 8.

Example 4 Find the difference between 32 and 17.

Which is the greater of 32 and 17? Clearly 32 is the greater. Therefore we subtract 17 from 32.

```
 32
 17
 —
 15
 —
```

In the units column we cannot take 7 from 2. However if we borrow 1 from the tens place and put it before the 2 we get 12, the 3 in the tens column becoming 2. Now 7 from 12 leaves 5. We write 5 in the tens column of the answer and take 1 from 2 in the tens column leaving 1.

Many people find it easier to work the borrowing method the other way round and to write the subtraction out in this way:

```
 32
 17
  1
 —
 15
 —
```

We say that 7 from 2 will not go, so we take 7 from 12 giving 5 which we write in the units column of the answer. We now increase the 1 in the tens column by 1 making it 2 (the small figure 1 is a useful aid to the memory until practice makes it unnecessary). Finally we take 2 from 3 leaving 1 which is written in the tens column of the answer.

Example 5 Subtract 1835 from 5423.

```
 5423
 1835
  1 1 1
 ——
 3588
 ——
```

In the units column 5 from 3 will not go, so take 5 from 13 leaving 8. Increase the 3 on the bottom of the tens column by 1 making it 4. 4 from 2 will not go, so take 4 from 12 leaving 8 and increase the 8 on the bottom of the hundreds column by 1 making it 9. 9 from 4 will not go, so take 9 from 14 leaving 5. Finally increase the 1 on the bottom of the thousands column and take 2 from 5 leaving 3.

Exercise 3

1) Find the difference between 27 and 59.
2) Subtract 258 from 593.
3) Find the value of $53 - 39$.
4) Subtract 7693 from 9251.
5) What is the difference between 336 and 9562?

Combined Addition and Subtraction

Suppose we want to find the value of:
$$18 + 7 - 5 + 3 - 16 + 8$$
we pick out all the numbers preceded by a plus sign and add them together. Thus:
$$18 + 7 + 3 + 8 = 36$$

(Note that the first number, it is 18, has no sign in front of it. When this happens a plus sign is always assumed.)

Next we pick out all the numbers preceded by a minus sign and add these together. Thus :
$$-5-16 = -21$$
Finally we subtract 21 from 36 to give 15.

Hence,
$$18+7-5+3-16+8 = 36-21 = 15$$

Example 6 Find the value of $2+6-3+9-5+11$.

$$2+6+9+11 = +28$$
$$-3-5 = -8$$

$$\begin{array}{r} 28 \\ \underline{8} \\ 20 \end{array} \right\} \text{Subtracting}$$

Exercise 4
Find the value of each of the following:

1) $8-6+7-5+9-2$
2) $21+32-63-58+79+32-11$
3) $152-78+43-81$
4) $27+45+9+7-15-23-41-8+17$

Arithmetical Signs, Terms and Symbols

The result obtained by adding numbers is called the *sum*. Thus the sum of 9 and 6 is 15.

The result obtained by subtracting one number from another is called the *difference*. The difference between 19 and 8 is $19-8 = 11$.

The sign $=$ is the sign of *equality* and means equal to. Thus 4 hours $=$ 240 minutes.

$+$ is the *addition* sign meaning plus. Thus $4+5 = 9$

$-$ is the *subtraction* sign meaning minus. Thus $9-5 = 4$

$\times$ is the *multiplication* sign meaning multiplied by, or times. Thus $6 \times 8 = 48$

$\div$ is the *division* sign meaning divided by. There are several ways of indicating division which are as follows:

1) $6 \div 3 = 2$ This reads six divided by three equals two.
2) $\dfrac{6}{3} = 2$ This reads six over three (or six divided by three) equals two.
3) $3\overline{)6} \atop 2$ This reads three into six goes two or six divided by three equals two.

Multiplication

We can find the value of $6+6+6+6$ by adding the four sixes together. The answer is 24. We could, however, do this more rapidly by using the multiplication tables because we know that $4 \times 6 = 24$.

When two numbers are multiplied together the result is called the *product*. Thus the product of 5 and 9 is $5 \times 9 = 45$.

MULTIPLICATION TABLE

1	2	3	4	5	6	7	8	9	10
2	4	6	8	10	12	14	16	18	20
3	6	9	12	15	18	21	24	27	30
4	8	12	16	20	24	28	32	36	40
5	10	15	20	25	30	35	40	45	50
6	12	18	24	30	36	42	48	54	60
7	14	21	28	35	42	49	56	63	70
8	16	24	32	40	48	56	64	72	80
9	18	27	36	45	54	63	72	81	90
10	20	30	40	50	60	70	80	90	100

The multiplication table is shown above. The extreme left hand vertical column, 1 to 10, as well as the top horizontal row, give the numbers whose products we wish to find. Thus to find the product of 6 and 8 (i.e. 6×8) we find 6 in the extreme left hand column. We then run the eye, or a finger, horizontally along this row until we come to the column headed 8 and we find the number 48, which is the required product. Hence $6 \times 8 = 48$. Similarly we find that $5 \times 9 = 45$ and $9 \times 8 = 72$.

You should use this multiplication table to revise the tables you may previously have studied. Try to make sure that you know up to 10×10 without the need to refer to the table.

Exercise 5

Write down the following products:

1) 3×2
2) 5×7
3) 9×6
4) 8×4
5) 7×9
6) 5×3
7) 9×9
8) 6×7

Long Multiplication

Example 7 Multiply 236 by 7.

```
 236
   7
————
1652
```

7 times 6 is 42. Place the 2 in the answer and carry the 4. 7 times 3 is 21, plus the 4 carried, is 25. Place 5 in the answer and carry the 2. 7 times 2 is 14, plus the 2 carried is 16.

OPERATIONS IN ARITHMETIC

Example 8   Multiply 369 by 527.

```
   369
   527
  ────
  2583
   738
  1845
  ──────
  194463
  ──────
```

Write the two numbers with their respective units figures directly underneath each other. Start by multiplying 369 by 7 giving 2583. Write the 3 directly beneath the units figures of the two numbers to be multiplied together. Now multiply 369 by 2 (which is really 20) giving 738. Make sure that the figures obtained by multiplying are this time moved one place to the left. Finally, when multiplying by 5 (which is really 500) it is again necessary to move one further place to the left. We now add the three sets of figures obtained by multiplication, the result being 194 463.

Alternatively if you wish, you can start with the left-hand figure in the multiplier as shown:

```
   369
   527
  ──────
  184500
    7380
    2583
  ──────
  194463
  ──────
```

First multiply 369 by 500 giving 184 500. Then multiply 369 by 20 giving 7380 and finally multiply 369 by 7 giving 2583. To obtain the product add these three sets of figures obtained by multiplication.

Checking the Accuracy of a Multiplication

There is a simple method of checking the result of a multiplication which is illustrated by considering:

$$843 \times 797 = 671\,871$$

Sum of the digits of $843 = 8+4+3 = 15$; $15 \div 9 = 1$ and remainder 6
Sum of the digits of $797 = 7+9+7 = 23$; $23 \div 9 = 2$ and remainder 5
Multiplying the remainders: $6 \times 5 = 30$; $30 \div 9 = 3$ and remainder 3
Sum of the digits of the product =
$\qquad 6+7+1+8+7+1 = 30$; $30 \div 9 = 3$ and remainder 3
Since the two remainders are the same the product 671 871 is correct.

Example 9   Multiply 369 by 527 and check the accuracy of the multiplication.

This multiplication has already been performed in Example 8 and we find that:

$$369 \times 527 = 194\,463.$$

Sum of the digits of $369 = 3+6+9 = 18$; $18 \div 9 = 2$ and remainder 0
Sum of the digits of $527 = 5+2+7 = 14$; $14 \div 9 = 1$ and remainder 5
Multiplying the remainders: $0 \times 5 = 0$
Sum of the digits of the product =
$\qquad 1+9+4+4+6+3 = 27$; $27 \div 9 = 3$ and remainder 0
Since the two remainders are the same the product is correct.

Exercise 6

Obtain the following products and check your accuracy:

1) 29×32
2) 359×26
3) 3149×321
4) 5683×789
5) 17632×58

Division

Division consists of finding how many times one number is contained in another number.

The *dividend* is the number to be divided.

The *divisor* is the number by which the dividend is divided.

The *quotient* is the result of the division.

Thus, $\dfrac{\text{dividend}}{\text{divisor}} = \text{quotient}$

Short Division

If the divisor is less than 10 it is usual to work by short division.

Example 10   Divide 2625 by 7.

7)2625   7 will not divide into 2. Next try 7 into 26. It goes 3 and a
  375   remainder of 5. Carry the remainder so that the next number to be divided is 52. 7 goes into 52, 7 times and remainder 3. Carry the 3 so that the next number to be divided is 35. 7 into 35 goes 5 exactly.

Example 11   Divide 1979 by 9.

9)1979   9 will not divide into 1 so try dividing 9 into
  219 remainder 8   19. It goes 2 remainder 1. Carry the 1 so that the next number to be divided is 17. 9 into 17 goes 1 remainder 8. Carry the 8 so that the next number to be divided is 89. 9 goes into 89 9 remainder 8. There are no more numbers to divide so the answer is 219 remainder 8.

Exercise 7

Work out the answers to the following:

1) $1968 \div 8$
2) $392 \div 7$
3) $2168 \div 5$
4) $7369 \div 4$
5) $5621 \div 9$

Long Division

The method is shown in the next example.

Example 12   Divide 3024 by 36.

```
36)3024(84
   288
   ---
   144
   144
   ---
   ...
```
36 consists of two digits. Look at the first two digits in the dividend, i.e. 30. 36 will not divide into 30 because 36 is the larger number. Next look at the first three figures of the dividend. They are 302. Will 36 divide into 302? It will because 302 is the larger number. How many times will it go? Let us multiply 36 by 9 the result is 324 which is greater than 302. Now try 36×8. The result is 288 which is less than 302. Place 8 in the answer (i.e. the quotient) and write the 288 under the 302. Subtracting 288 from 302 we get a remainder of 14. Now bring down the next figure in the dividend, which is 4. Now divide 36 into 144. The result is 4 exactly because $4 \times 36 = 144$. Write 4 in the quotient and we see that $3024 \div 36 = 84$ exactly.

Example 13 Divide 1 000 000 by 250.

```
250)1000000(4000
    1000
    ----
    ....
```
250 will not divide into the first three figures of the dividend (100) so we try 250 into 1000. It goes 4 times exactly leaving no remainder. To obtain the quotient the remaining three zeros are written in the quotient giving 4000.

Tests for Divisibility

A number is divisible by:

2 if it is an even number,

3 if the sum of the digits is divisible by 3 (3156 is divisible by 3 because $3+1+5+6 = 15$ which is divisible by 3),

4 if its last two figures are divisible by 4 (3024 is divisible by 4 because $24 \div 4 = 6$ exactly),

5 if its last figure is zero or five (3265 and 4280 are both divisible by 5),

10 if its last figure is zero (198 630 is divisible by 10).

Exercise 8

Work out the answers to the following:

1) $4918 \div 9$
2) $7584 \div 6$
3) $1237 \div 4$
4) $10001 \div 11$
5) $15352 \div 17$
6) $45927 \div 27$
7) $2093595 \div 35$
8) $290227 \div 49$

Sequence of Arithmetical Operations

Numbers are often combined in a series of arithmetical operations. When this happens a definite sequence must be observed.

1) Brackets are used if there is any danger of ambiguity. The contents of the bracket must be evaluated before performing any other operation. Thus:

$$2 \times (7+4) = 2 \times 11 = 22$$
$$15 - (8-3) = 15 - 5 = 10$$

2) Multiplication and division must be done before addition and subtraction. Thus;
$$5\times8+7 = 40+7 = 47 \text{ (not } 5\times15)$$
$$8\div4+9 = 2+9 = 11 \text{ (not } 8\div13)$$
$$5\times4-12\div3+7 = 20-4+7 = 27-4 = 23$$

Exercise 9

Find values for the following:

1) $3+5\times2$
2) $3\times6-8$
3) $7\times5-2+4\times6$
4) $8\div2+3$
5) $7\times5-12\div4+3$
6) $11-9\div3+7$
7) $3\times(8+7)$
8) $2+8\times(3+6)$
9) $17-2\times(5-3)$
10) $11-12\div4+3\times(6-2)$

Mental Test 1

Try to answer the following questions without writing anything down except the answer.

1) Add 3, 7, 4, 9 and 5.
2) Add 2, 4, 6, 8, 10 and 12.
3) Add 20, 30, 40, 50, 60, 70 and 80.
4) Add 12, 15 and 19.
5) Subtract 17 from 28.
6) Take 14 away from 23.
7) Find the sum of 27 and 35.
8) Add 19 and 13 and take away 27 from the sum.
9) Find the difference between 29 and 54.
10) Multiply 13 by 5.
11) Find the product of 14 and 6.
12) Multiply 19 by 7.
13) Multiply 273 by 3.
14) Divide 63 by 3.
15) Divide 515 by 5.
16) Multiply 311 by 9.
17) Add 126, 37 and 54.
18) Divide 572 by 4.
19) Multiply 17 by 5 and then add 23.
20) Divide 164 by 4 and then take away 18.

Self-Test 1

In questions 1 to 4 state the letter corresponding to the correct answer.

1) Thirty thousand and four in figures is:
   a 3004   **b** 30004
   c 34000   **d** 30400
   e 300004

2) Five thousand and fifteen in figures is:
   a 5015   **b** 5150
   c 5115   **d** 50015
   e 515

3) One hundred and six thousand and sixteen in figures is:
   a 116000   **b** 106000
   c 106160   **d** 116160
   e 106016

4) Ten million, seventeen thousand and six in figures is:
   a 10017006   **b** 10170006
   c 10017060   **d** 10017600
   e 10170060

5) Add up the three sets of figures below:

(a)	(b)	(c)
5018	3263	528
362	8783	5079
12894	35	9867
268	357	61
4134	10089	356

OPERATIONS IN ARITHMETIC

6) State the letter corresponding to correct answer to the problems shown below.

(a) $107-104+63-48+137+50-149$
 a 65 **b** 56 **c** 66

(b) $368-55+378-286+245-254$
 a 416 **b** 395 **c** 396

(c) $45-764+418-382+1049-689+1000$
 a 677 **b** 605 **c** 687

7) Subtract the following:
(a) $2092-987$
(b) $2315-999$
(c) $7005-889$
(d) $958-697$
(e) $432-318$
(f) $23\,301-22\,398$

8) Multiply the following:
(a) $16\,398 \times 7$
(b) $635\,489 \times 12$
(c) $93\,081 \times 407$
(d) $51\,365 \times 450$
(e) 9457×6003
(f) $68\,859 \times 836$

9) Divide the following:
(a) $46\,348 \div 4$
(b) $32\,340 \div 60$
(c) $1536 \div 32$
(d) $17\,280 \div 960$

10) In each of the following division problems there is a remainder. Perform the division and state the remainder:
(a) $685\,329 \div 64$
(b) $61\,385 \div 13$
(c) $969\,234 \div 19$
(d) $17\,432 \div 560$

11) Each of the following numbers is divisible by either 4, 8, 16, 5, 10, 9 or 11. State which number will divide exactly into the given number:
(a) 1404
(b) 8615
(c) 4167
(d) 1564
(e) 102 971
(f) 73 216

12) State the letter corresponding to the correct answer to the problems shown below.

(a) $3+7 \times 4$
 a 40 **b** 31 **c** 84

(b) $6 \times 5 - 2 + 4 \times 6$
 a 52 **b** 42 **c** 18

(c) $7 \times 6 - 12 \div 3 + 1$
 a 40 **b** 39 **c** 21

(d) $17 - 2 \times (6-4)$
 a 30 **b** 1 **c** 13

(e) $3 \times 5 - 12 \div (3+1)$
 a 12 **b** 10 **c** 8

In questions 13 to 20 decide if the answer is true or false and write the correct answer in your notebook.

13) $7 + 5 \times 3 = 22$
14) $7 - 2 \times 3 = 15$
15) $6 \times 5 - 3 + 2 \times 7 = 26$
16) $10 \div 2 + 3 = 8$
17) $7 \times 5 - 12 \div 4 + 2 = 10$
18) $18 - 10 \div 2 + 3 \times (5-2) = 22$
19) $36 - 27 + 54 - 58 = 15$
20) The exact value of,
 $(312 \times 11 \times 19) \div 39$ is 1672

2. Fractions

UNDERSTAND THE FOUR BASIC RULES OF ARITHMETIC
Define numerator and denominator of a fraction.
Simplify fractions by cancellation.
Connect mixed numbers to improper fractions and vice versa.
Perform both written and mental calculations involving addition, subtraction, multiplication and division of fractions.

Introduction

In this chapter we deal with the rules for the addition, subtraction, multiplication and division of fractions.

Vulgar Fractions

The circle in Fig. 2.1 has been divided into eight equal parts. Each part is called one-eighth of the circle and is written as $\frac{1}{8}$. The number 8 below the line shows how many equal parts there are and it is called the *denominator*. The number above the line shows how many of the equal parts are taken and it is called the *numerator*. If five of the eight equal parts are taken then we have taken $\frac{5}{8}$ of the circle.

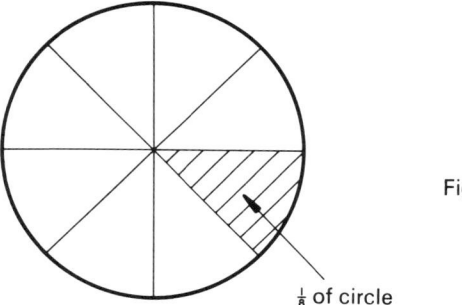

Fig. 2.1

$\frac{1}{8}$ of circle

From what has been said above we see that a fraction is always a part of something. The number below the line (the denominator) gives the fraction its name and tells us the number of equal parts into which the whole has been divided. The top number (the numerator) tells us the number of these equal parts that are to be taken. For example the fraction $\frac{3}{4}$ means that the whole has been divided into four equal parts and that three of these parts are to be taken.

The value of a fraction is unchanged if we multiply or divide both its numerator and denominator by the same amount.

$\frac{3}{5} = \frac{12}{20}$ (by multiplying the numerator and denominator by 4)

$\frac{2}{7} = \frac{10}{35}$ (by multiplying the numerator and denominator by 5)

FRACTIONS

$$\frac{12}{32} = \frac{3}{8} \text{ (by dividing the numerator and denominator by 4)}$$

$$\frac{16}{64} = \frac{1}{4} \text{ (by dividing the numerator and denominator by 16)}$$

Example 1 Write down the fraction $\frac{2}{7}$ with a denominator of 28.

In order to make the denominator 28, we must multiply the original denominator of 7 by 4 because $7 \times 4 = 28$. Remembering that to leave the value of the fraction unchanged we must multiply both numerator and denominator by the same amount, then:

$$\frac{2}{7} = \frac{2 \times 4}{7 \times 4} = \frac{8}{28}$$

Exercise 10

Write down the following fractions with the denominator stated:

1) $\frac{3}{4}$ with denominator 28

2) $\frac{3}{5}$ with denominator 20

3) $\frac{5}{6}$ with denominator 30

4) $\frac{1}{9}$ with denominator 63

5) $\frac{2}{3}$ with denominator 12

6) $\frac{1}{6}$ with denominator 24

7) $\frac{3}{8}$ with denominator 64

8) $\frac{5}{7}$ with denominator 35

Reducing a Fraction to its Lowest Terms

Fractions like $\frac{3}{8}$, $\frac{7}{16}$ and $\frac{5}{32}$ are said to be in their *lowest terms* because it is impossible to find a number which will divide exactly into both the numerator and denominator. However, fractions like $\frac{9}{18}$, $\frac{8}{12}$ and $\frac{21}{24}$ are not in their lowest terms because they can be reduced further by dividing both numerator and denominator by some number which divides exactly into both of them. Thus:

$$\frac{9}{18} = \frac{1}{2} \text{ (by dividing both numerator and denominator by 9)}$$

$$\frac{8}{12} = \frac{2}{3} \text{ (by dividing both numerator and denominator by 4)}.$$

$$\frac{21}{24} = \frac{7}{8} \text{ (by dividing both numerator and denominator by 3)}$$

Sometimes we can divide the numerator and denominator by the same number several times.

Example 2 Reduce $\frac{210}{336}$ to its lowest terms.

$$\frac{210}{336} = \frac{105}{168} \text{ (by dividing top and bottom by 2)}$$
$$= \frac{35}{56} \text{ (by dividing top and bottom by 3)}$$
$$= \frac{5}{8} \text{ (by dividing top and bottom by 7)}$$

Hence $\frac{210}{336}$ reduced to its lowest terms is $\frac{5}{8}$

Exercise 11

Reduce the following fractions to their lowest terms:

1) $\frac{8}{16}$
2) $\frac{9}{15}$
3) $\frac{8}{64}$
4) $\frac{15}{25}$
5) $\frac{42}{48}$
6) $\frac{180}{240}$
7) $\frac{210}{294}$
8) $\frac{126}{245}$
9) $\frac{132}{198}$
10) $\frac{210}{315}$

Types of Fractions

If the numerator of a fraction is less than its denominator the fraction is called a *proper fraction*. Thus, $\frac{2}{3}$, $\frac{5}{8}$ and $\frac{3}{4}$ are all proper fractions. Note that a proper fraction has a value which is less than 1.

If the numerator of a fraction is greater than its denominator then the fraction is called an *improper fraction* or a *top heavy fraction*. Thus, $\frac{5}{4}$, $\frac{3}{2}$ and $\frac{9}{7}$ are all top heavy, or improper, fractions. Note that all top heavy fractions have a value which is greater than 1.

Every top heavy fraction can be expressed as a whole number and a proper fraction. These are sometimes called *mixed numbers*. Thus $1\frac{1}{2}$, $5\frac{1}{3}$ and $9\frac{3}{4}$ are all mixed numbers. In order to convert a top heavy fraction into a mixed number it must be remembered that:

$$\frac{\text{numerator}}{\text{denominator}} = \text{numerator} \div \text{denominator}$$

Example 3   Express $\frac{15}{8}$ as a mixed number.

$$\frac{15}{8} = 1\frac{7}{8} \text{ (because } 15 \div 8 = 1 \text{ and remainder 7)}$$

From Example 3 we see that we convert a top heavy fraction into a mixed number by dividing the denominator into the numerator. Notice that the remainder becomes the numerator in the fractional part of the mixed number. To change a mixed number into an improper fraction we multiply the whole number by the denominator of the fractional part. To this we add the numerator of the fractional part and this sum then becomes the numerator of the improper fraction. Its denominator is the same as the denominator of the fractional part of the mixed number.

FRACTIONS

Example 4 Express $3\frac{5}{8}$ as a top heavy fraction.

$$3\frac{5}{8} = \frac{(8 \times 3)+5}{8} = \frac{24+5}{8} = \frac{29}{8}$$

Exercise 12

Express each of the following as a mixed number:

1) $\frac{7}{2}$

2) $\frac{8}{4}$

3) $\frac{22}{10}$

4) $\frac{12}{11}$

5) $\frac{21}{8}$

Express each of the following as top-heavy fractions:

6) $2\frac{3}{8}$

7) $5\frac{1}{10}$

8) $8\frac{2}{3}$

9) $6\frac{7}{20}$

10) $4\frac{3}{7}$

Lowest Common Multiple (LCM)

The LCM of a set of numbers is the *smallest* number into which each of the given numbers will divide. Thus the LCM of 4, 5 and 10 is 20 because 20 is the smallest number into which the numbers 4, 5 and 10 will divide exactly.

The LCM of a set of numbers can usually be found by inspection.

Exercise 13

Find the LCM of the following sets of numbers:

1) 8 and 12
2) 3, 4 and 5
3) 2, 6 and 12
4) 3, 6 and 8
5) 2, 8 and 10
6) 20 and 25
7) 20 and 32
8) 10, 15 and 40
9) 12, 42, 60 and 70
10) 18, 30, 42 and 48

Lowest Common Denominator

When we wish to compare the values of two or more fractions the easiest way is to express the fractions with the same denominator. This common denominator should be the LCM of the denominators of the fractions to be compared and it is called the *lowest common denominator*.

Example 5 Arrange the fractions $\frac{3}{4}, \frac{5}{8}, \frac{7}{10}$ and $\frac{11}{20}$ in order of size starting with the smallest.

The lowest common denominator of 4, 8, 10 and 20 is 40. Expressing each of the given fractions with a denominator of 40 gives:

$$\frac{3}{4} = \frac{3 \times 10}{4 \times 10} = \frac{30}{40} \qquad \frac{5}{8} = \frac{5 \times 5}{8 \times 5} = \frac{25}{40}$$

$$\frac{7}{10} = \frac{7 \times 4}{10 \times 4} = \frac{28}{40} \qquad \frac{11}{20} = \frac{11 \times 2}{20 \times 2} = \frac{22}{40}$$

Therefore the order is $\frac{22}{40}, \frac{25}{40}, \frac{28}{40}, \frac{30}{40}$ or $\frac{11}{20}, \frac{5}{8}, \frac{7}{10}$ and $\frac{3}{4}$

Exercise 14

Arrange the following sets of fractions in order of size, beginning with the smallest:

1) $\frac{1}{2}, \frac{5}{6}, \frac{2}{3}, \frac{7}{12}$

2) $\frac{9}{10}, \frac{3}{4}, \frac{6}{7}, \frac{7}{8}$

3) $\frac{13}{16}, \frac{11}{20}, \frac{7}{10}, \frac{3}{5}$

4) $\frac{3}{4}, \frac{5}{8}, \frac{3}{5}, \frac{13}{20}$

5) $\frac{11}{16}, \frac{7}{10}, \frac{9}{14}, \frac{3}{4}$

6) $\frac{3}{8}, \frac{4}{7}, \frac{5}{9}, \frac{2}{5}$

Addition of Fractions

The steps when adding fractions are as follows:

(1) Find the lowest common denominator of the fractions to be added.
(2) Express each of the fractions with this common denominator.
(3) Add the numerators of the new fractions to give the numerator of the answer. The denominator of the answer is the lowest common denominator found in (1).

Example 6   Find the sum of $\frac{2}{7}$ and $\frac{3}{4}$.

First find the lowest common denominator (this is the LCM of 7 and 4). It is 28. Now express $\frac{2}{7}$ and $\frac{3}{4}$ with a denominator of 28.

$$\frac{2}{7} = \frac{2 \times 4}{7 \times 4} = \frac{8}{28} \qquad \frac{3}{4} = \frac{3 \times 7}{4 \times 7} = \frac{21}{28}$$

Adding the numerators of the new fractions:

$$\frac{2}{7} + \frac{3}{4} = \frac{8}{28} + \frac{21}{28} = \frac{29}{28} = 1\frac{1}{28}$$

A better way of setting out the work is as follows:

$$\frac{2}{7} + \frac{3}{4} = \frac{2 \times 4 + 3 \times 7}{28} = \frac{8 + 21}{28} = \frac{29}{28} = 1\frac{1}{28}$$

FRACTIONS

Example 7 Simplify $\frac{3}{4}+\frac{2}{3}+\frac{7}{10}$.

The LCM of the denominators 4, 3 and 10 is 60.

$$\frac{3}{4}+\frac{2}{3}+\frac{7}{10} = \frac{3\times15+2\times20+7\times6}{60} = \frac{45+40+42}{60} = \frac{127}{60} = 2\frac{7}{60}$$

Example 8 Add together $5\frac{1}{2}$, $2\frac{2}{3}$ and $3\frac{2}{5}$.

First add the whole numbers together, $5+2+3 = 10$. Then add the fractional parts in the usual way. The LCM of 2, 3 and 5 is 30.

$$5\frac{1}{2}+2\frac{2}{3}+3\frac{2}{5} = 10+\frac{15\times1+10\times2+6\times2}{30} = 10+\frac{15+20+12}{30}$$

$$= 10+\frac{47}{30} = 10+1\frac{17}{30} = 11\frac{17}{30}$$

Exercise 15

Add together:

1) $\frac{1}{2}+\frac{1}{3}$

2) $\frac{2}{5}+\frac{9}{10}$

3) $\frac{3}{4}+\frac{3}{8}$

4) $\frac{3}{10}+\frac{1}{4}$

5) $\frac{1}{2}+\frac{3}{4}+\frac{7}{8}$

6) $\frac{1}{8}+\frac{2}{3}+\frac{3}{5}$

7) $1\frac{3}{8}+3\frac{9}{16}$

8) $7\frac{2}{3}+6\frac{3}{5}$

9) $3\frac{3}{8}+5\frac{2}{7}+4\frac{3}{4}$

10) $4\frac{1}{2}+3\frac{5}{6}+2\frac{1}{3}$

11) $7\frac{3}{8}+2\frac{3}{4}+\frac{7}{8}+\frac{5}{16}$

12) $7\frac{2}{3}+\frac{2}{5}+\frac{3}{10}+2\frac{1}{2}$

Subtraction of Fractions

The method is similar to that used in addition. Find the common denominator of the fractions and after expressing each fraction with this common denominator, subtract.

Example 9 Simplify $\frac{5}{8}-\frac{2}{5}$.

The LCM of the denominators is 40.

$$\frac{5}{8}-\frac{2}{5} = \frac{5\times5-8\times2}{40} = \frac{25-16}{40} = \frac{9}{40}$$

When mixed numbers have to be subtracted the best way is to turn the mixed numbers into top heavy fractions and then proceed in the way shown in Example 9.

Example 10 Simplify $3\frac{7}{10}-2\frac{3}{4}$.

$$3\frac{7}{10}-2\frac{3}{4} = \frac{37}{10}-\frac{11}{4} = \frac{37\times2-11\times5}{20} = \frac{74-55}{20} = \frac{19}{20}$$

Example 11 Simplify $5\frac{2}{5}-3\frac{7}{8}$.

$$5\frac{2}{5}-3\frac{7}{8} = \frac{27}{5}-\frac{31}{8} = \frac{27\times 8-31\times 5}{40} = \frac{216-155}{40} = \frac{61}{40} = 1\frac{21}{40}$$

Exercise 16

Simplify the following:

1) $\frac{1}{2}-\frac{1}{3}$

2) $\frac{1}{3}-\frac{1}{5}$

3) $\frac{2}{3}-\frac{1}{2}$

4) $\frac{7}{8}-\frac{3}{8}$

5) $\frac{7}{8}-\frac{5}{6}$

6) $3\frac{1}{4}-2\frac{3}{8}$

7) $3-\frac{5}{7}$

8) $5-3\frac{4}{5}$

9) $5\frac{3}{8}-2\frac{9}{10}$

10) $4\frac{7}{32}-3\frac{9}{10}$

11) $1\frac{5}{16}-\frac{4}{5}$

Combined Addition and Subtraction

Example 12 Simplify $5\frac{3}{8}-1\frac{1}{4}+2\frac{1}{2}-\frac{7}{16}$.

$$5\frac{3}{8}-1\frac{1}{4}+2\frac{1}{2}-\frac{7}{16} = \frac{43}{8}-\frac{5}{4}+\frac{5}{2}-\frac{7}{16} = \frac{43\times 2-5\times 4+5\times 8-7\times 1}{16}$$

$$= \frac{86-20+40-7}{16} = \frac{(86+40)-(20+7)}{16}$$

$$= \frac{126-27}{16} = \frac{99}{16} = 6\frac{3}{16}$$

Exercise 17

Simplify the following:

1) $2\frac{1}{2}+3\frac{1}{4}-4\frac{3}{8}$

2) $5\frac{1}{10}-3\frac{1}{2}-1\frac{1}{4}$

3) $4\frac{3}{8}-2\frac{1}{2}+5$

4) $6\frac{1}{2}-3\frac{1}{6}+2\frac{1}{12}-4\frac{3}{4}$

5) $1\frac{3}{16}-2\frac{2}{5}+3\frac{3}{4}+5\frac{5}{8}$

6) $12\frac{7}{10}-5\frac{1}{8}+3\frac{3}{20}+1\frac{1}{2}$

7) $2\frac{3}{16}-2\frac{3}{10}+\frac{5}{8}+1\frac{3}{4}$

8) $12\frac{3}{4}-6\frac{7}{8}+5\frac{21}{32}-2\frac{13}{16}$

9) $3\frac{9}{20}+1\frac{3}{8}-2\frac{7}{10}+1\frac{3}{4}$

10) $2\frac{9}{25}+3\frac{4}{5}-2\frac{7}{10}-\frac{3}{20}$

Multiplication

When multiplying together two or more fractions we first multiply all the numerators together and then we multiply all the denominators together. Mixed numbers must always be converted into top heavy fractions.

FRACTIONS

Example 13   Simplify $\frac{5}{8} \times \frac{3}{7}$

$$\frac{5}{8} \times \frac{3}{7} = \frac{5 \times 3}{8 \times 7} = \frac{15}{56}$$

Example 14   Simplify $\frac{2}{5} \times 3\frac{2}{3}$

$$\frac{2}{5} \times 3\frac{2}{3} = \frac{2}{5} \times \frac{11}{3} = \frac{2 \times 11}{5 \times 3} = \frac{22}{15} = 1\frac{7}{15}$$

Example 15   Simplify $1\frac{3}{8} \times 1\frac{1}{4}$

$$1\frac{3}{8} \times 1\frac{1}{4} = \frac{11}{8} \times \frac{5}{4} = \frac{11 \times 5}{8 \times 4} = \frac{55}{32} = 1\frac{23}{32}$$

Exercise 18

Simplify the following:

1) $\frac{2}{3} \times \frac{4}{5}$ 3) $\frac{2}{9} \times 1\frac{2}{3}$ 5) $1\frac{2}{5} \times 3\frac{1}{2}$ 7) $1\frac{2}{9} \times 1\frac{2}{5}$

2) $\frac{3}{4} \times \frac{5}{7}$ 4) $\frac{5}{9} \times \frac{11}{4}$ 6) $2\frac{1}{2} \times 2\frac{2}{3}$ 8) $1\frac{7}{8} \times 1\frac{4}{7}$

Cancelling

Example 16   Simplify $\frac{2}{3} \times 1\frac{7}{8}$

$$\frac{2}{3} \times 1\frac{7}{8} = \frac{2}{3} \times \frac{15}{8} = \frac{2 \times 15}{3 \times 8} = \frac{30}{24} = \frac{5}{4} = 1\frac{1}{4}$$

The step to reducing $\frac{30}{24}$ to its lowest terms has been done by dividing 6 into both the numerator and denominator.

The work can be made easier by *cancelling* before multiplication as shown below.

$$\frac{\overset{1}{\cancel{2}}}{\cancel{3}} \times \frac{\overset{5}{\cancel{15}}}{\cancel{8}} = \frac{1 \times 5}{1 \times 4} = \frac{5}{4} = 1\frac{1}{4}$$

We have divided 2 into 2 (a numerator) and 8 (a denominator) and also we have divided 3 into 15 (a numerator) and 3 (a denominator). You will see that we have divided the numerators and the denominators by the same amount. Notice carefully that we can only cancel between a numerator and a denominator.

Example 17   Simplify $\frac{16}{25} \times \frac{7}{8} \times 8\frac{3}{4}$

$$\frac{\cancel{16}^{\,2\,\,1}}{\cancel{25}_{\,5}} \times \frac{7}{\cancel{8}_{\,1}} \times \frac{\cancel{35}^{\,7}}{\cancel{4}_{\,2}} = \frac{1 \times 7 \times 7}{5 \times 1 \times 2} = \frac{49}{10} = 4\frac{9}{10}$$

Sometimes in calculations with fractions the word 'of' appears. It should always be taken as meaning multiply. Thus

$$\frac{4}{5} \text{ of } 20 = \frac{4}{\cancel{5}_{\,1}} \times \frac{\cancel{20}^{\,4}}{1} = \frac{4 \times 4}{1 \times 1} = \frac{16}{1} = 16$$

Exercise 19

Simplify the following:

1) $\frac{3}{4} \times 1\frac{7}{9}$

2) $5\frac{1}{5} \times \frac{10}{13}$

3) $1\frac{5}{8} \times \frac{7}{26}$

4) $1\frac{1}{2} \times \frac{2}{5} \times 2\frac{1}{2}$

5) $\frac{5}{8} \times \frac{7}{10} \times \frac{2}{21}$

6) $2 \times 1\frac{1}{2} \times 1\frac{1}{3}$

7) $3\frac{3}{4} \times 1\frac{3}{5} \times 1\frac{1}{8}$

8) $\frac{15}{32} \times \frac{8}{11} \times 24\frac{1}{5}$

9) $\frac{3}{4}$ of 16

10) $\frac{5}{7}$ of 140

11) $\frac{2}{3}$ of $4\frac{1}{2}$

12) $\frac{4}{5}$ of $2\frac{1}{2}$

Division of Fractions

To divide by a fraction, all we have to do is to invert it and multiply. Thus:

$$\frac{3}{5} \div \frac{2}{7} = \frac{3}{5} \times \frac{7}{2} = \frac{3 \times 7}{5 \times 2} = \frac{21}{10} = 2\frac{1}{10}$$

Example 18 Divide $1\frac{4}{5}$ by $2\frac{1}{3}$

$$1\frac{4}{5} \div 2\frac{1}{3} = \frac{9}{5} \div \frac{7}{3} = \frac{9}{5} \times \frac{3}{7} = \frac{27}{35}$$

Exercise 20

Simplify the following:

1) $\frac{4}{5} \div 1\frac{1}{3}$

2) $2 \div \frac{1}{4}$

3) $\frac{5}{8} \div \frac{15}{32}$

4) $3\frac{3}{4} \div 2\frac{1}{2}$

5) $2\frac{1}{2} \div 3\frac{3}{4}$

6) $5 \div 5\frac{1}{5}$

7) $3\frac{1}{15} \div 2\frac{5}{9}$

8) $2\frac{3}{10} \div \frac{3}{5}$

FRACTIONS

Operations with Fractions

The sequence of operations when dealing with fractions is the same as those used with whole numbers. They are, in order:

(1) Work out brackets.
(2) Multiply and divide.
(3) Add and subtract.

Example 19 Simplify $\frac{1}{5} \div \left(\frac{1}{3} \div \frac{1}{2}\right)$.

$$\frac{1}{5} \div \left(\frac{1}{3} \div \frac{1}{2}\right) = \frac{1}{5} \div \left(\frac{1}{3} \times \frac{2}{1}\right) = \frac{1}{5} \div \frac{2}{3} = \frac{1}{5} \times \frac{3}{2} = \frac{3}{10}$$

Example 20 Simplify $\dfrac{2\frac{4}{5} + 1\frac{1}{4}}{3\frac{3}{5}} - \dfrac{5}{16}$.

With problems of this kind it is best to work in stages as shown below:

$$2\frac{4}{5} + 1\frac{1}{4} = 3\frac{16+5}{20} = 3\frac{21}{20} = 4\frac{1}{20}$$

$$\frac{4\frac{1}{20}}{3\frac{3}{5}} = \frac{81}{20} \div \frac{18}{5} = \frac{81}{20} \times \frac{5}{18} = \frac{9}{8}$$

$$\frac{9}{8} - \frac{5}{16} = \frac{18-5}{16} = \frac{13}{16}$$

Exercise 21

Simplify the following:

1) $3\frac{3}{14} + \left(1\frac{1}{49} \times \frac{7}{10}\right)$

2) $\frac{1}{4} \div \left(\frac{1}{8} \times \frac{2}{5}\right)$

3) $1\frac{2}{3} \div \left(\frac{3}{5} \div \frac{9}{10}\right)$

4) $\left(1\frac{7}{8} \times 2\frac{2}{5}\right) - 3\frac{2}{3}$

5) $\dfrac{2\frac{2}{3} + 1\frac{1}{5}}{5\frac{4}{5}}$

6) $3\frac{2}{3} \div \left(\frac{2}{3} + \frac{4}{5}\right)$

7) $\dfrac{5\frac{3}{5} - 3\frac{1}{2} \times \frac{2}{3}}{2\frac{1}{3}}$

8) $\frac{2}{5} \times \left(\frac{2}{3} - \frac{1}{4}\right) + \frac{1}{2}$

9) $\dfrac{3\frac{9}{16} \times \frac{4}{9}}{2 + 6\frac{1}{4} \times 1\frac{1}{5}}$

10) $\dfrac{\frac{5}{9} - \frac{7}{15}}{1 - \left(\frac{5}{9} \times \frac{7}{15}\right)}$

Summary

1) The denominator (bottom number) gives the fraction its name and gives the number of equal parts into which the whole has been divided. The numerator (top number) gives the number of equal parts that are to be taken.

2) The value of a fraction remains unaltered if both the numerator and the denominator are multiplied or divided by the same number.

3) The LCM of a set of numbers is the smallest number into which each of the numbers of the set will divide exactly.
4) To compare the values of fractions which have different denominators express all the fractions with the lowest common denominator and then compare the numerators of the new fractions.
5) To add fractions express each of them with their lowest common denominator and then add the resulting numerators.
6) To multiply fractions multiply the numerators together and then multiply the denominators together.
7) To divide, invert the divisor and then proceed as in multiplication.
8) The sequence of operations when dealing with fractions is: (i) work out brackets; (ii) multiply and divide; (iii) add and subtract.

Mental Test 2

Try to write down the answer to the questions which follow without writing anything else.

1) Simplify $\frac{3}{8} + \frac{1}{4}$

2) Simplify $\frac{2}{5} + \frac{3}{20}$

3) Simplify $\frac{7}{10} - \frac{2}{5}$

4) Simplify $\frac{1}{2} + \frac{1}{4} + \frac{1}{8}$

5) Add $\frac{3}{4}$ to the difference of $\frac{5}{8}$ and $\frac{3}{8}$

6) Simplify $\frac{1}{2} + \frac{3}{4} - \frac{2}{3}$

7) Simplify $\frac{1}{2} \times \frac{1}{5}$

8) Simplify $\frac{2}{3} \times \frac{3}{7}$

9) Multiply $\frac{2}{5}$ and $\frac{15}{16}$

10) What is $\frac{2}{3}$ of 12?

11) Find $\frac{3}{4}$ of 16

12) Simplify $\frac{1}{4} \div 2$

13) Divide $\frac{1}{4}$ by $\frac{3}{4}$

14) Simplify $\frac{1}{4} \div \frac{1}{2}$

15) Simplify $\frac{2}{3} \div \frac{4}{5}$

Self-Test 2

In questions 1 to 15 state the letter, or letters, corresponding to the correct answer or answers.

1) When the fraction $\frac{630}{1470}$ is reduced to its lowest terms the answer is

   a $\frac{63}{147}$ b $\frac{3}{7}$ c $\frac{21}{49}$ d $\frac{9}{20}$

2) Which of the following fractions is equal to $\frac{4}{9}$?

   a $\frac{12}{27}$ b $\frac{4}{36}$ c $\frac{36}{4}$ d $\frac{20}{90}$ e $\frac{52}{117}$

3) The fraction $\frac{3}{4}$ when written with denominator 56 is the same as

   a $\frac{3}{56}$ b $\frac{56}{12}$ c $\frac{42}{56}$ d $\frac{56}{42}$

4) The LCM of 5, 15, 40 and 64 is
   a 960   b 192 000   c 640
   d 64

5) The mixed number $3\frac{5}{6}$ is equal to

   a $\frac{15}{6}$ b $\frac{5}{18}$ c $\frac{15}{18}$ d $\frac{23}{6}$

FRACTIONS

6) The improper fraction $\frac{104}{14}$ is equal to

a $7\frac{3}{7}$ b $\frac{364}{49}$ c $7\frac{6}{14}$ d $\frac{52}{7}$

7) $\frac{1}{4}+\frac{2}{3}+\frac{3}{5}$ is equal to

a $\frac{1}{2}$ b $\frac{1}{10}$ c $\frac{91}{60}$ d $1\frac{31}{60}$

8) $1\frac{3}{8}+2\frac{5}{6}+3\frac{1}{4}$ is equal to

a $6\frac{4}{9}$ b $6\frac{15}{192}$ c $\frac{35}{24}$ d $\frac{21}{40}$

e $7\frac{11}{24}$

9) $1\frac{1}{8}+2\frac{1}{6}+3\frac{3}{4}$ is equal to

a $6\frac{5}{18}$ b $7\frac{1}{24}$ c $1\frac{1}{24}$ d $7\frac{5}{24}$

10) $\frac{7}{8}\times\frac{3}{5}$ is equal to

a $\frac{10}{13}$ b $\frac{4}{3}$ c $\frac{35}{24}$ d $\frac{21}{40}$

11) $\frac{5}{8}\times\frac{4}{15}$ is equal to one of the following, when the answer is expressed in its lowest terms:

a $\frac{20}{120}$ b $\frac{1}{6}$ c $\frac{32}{75}$ d $\frac{9}{23}$

12) $\frac{3}{4}\div\frac{8}{9}$ is equal to

a $\frac{24}{36}$ b $\frac{2}{3}$ c $\frac{27}{32}$ d $\frac{3}{2}$

13) $6\frac{4}{9}\div 3\frac{2}{3}$ is equal to

a $2\frac{2}{3}$ b $\frac{638}{27}$ c $\frac{58}{33}$ d $18\frac{8}{27}$

14) $3\times\left(\frac{1}{2}-\frac{1}{3}\right)$ is equal to

a $1\frac{1}{2}-\frac{1}{3}$ b $\frac{1}{2}$

c $3\times\frac{1}{2}-3\times\frac{1}{3}$ d none of these

15) $\frac{5}{8}+\frac{1}{2}\times\frac{1}{4}$ is equal to

a $\frac{9}{32}$ b $\frac{3}{4}$ c $\frac{9}{16}$ d $\frac{3}{32}$

In questions 16 to 25 decide whether the answer given is true or false.

16) In a fraction the number above the line is called the numerator.

17) In a proper fraction the numerator is always greater than the denominator.

18) If the numerator of a fraction is greater than its denominator then the fraction is called an improper fraction.

19) An improper fraction always has a value greater than 1.

20) The fraction $6\frac{2}{5}$ is called a mixed number.

21) When the fractions $\frac{5}{8}, \frac{3}{4}, \frac{7}{10}$ and $\frac{3}{5}$ are put in order of size the result is $\frac{3}{5}, \frac{5}{8}, \frac{7}{10}$ and $\frac{3}{4}$.

22) $\frac{27}{9}$ is the same as $27\div 9$.

23) $\frac{28}{35}\div\frac{7}{16}$ is the same as $\frac{28}{35}\times\frac{16}{7}$.

24) $3\times(\frac{1}{2}+\frac{1}{4})$ is the same as $3\times\frac{3}{4}$.

25) $\frac{5}{8}+\frac{1}{4}\times\frac{1}{2}$ is the same as $\frac{7}{8}\times\frac{1}{2}$.

3. The Decimal System

UNDERSTAND THE FOUR BASIC RULES OF ARITHMETIC

Recognise a decimal fraction.
Convert decimals to fractions and vice versa.
Reduce a decimal to a given number of decimal places.
State a decimal to a given number of significant figures.

Introduction

In this chapter we first deal with the addition, subtraction, multiplication and division of decimal numbers. Then rough checks for calculations are discussed and finally the conversion of fractions to decimals and vice-versa are discussed.

The Decimal System

The decimal system is an extension of our ordinary number system. When we write the number 666 we mean $600+60+6$. Reading from left to right each figure 6 is ten times the value of the next one.

We now have to decide how to deal with fractional quantities, that is, quantities whose values are less than one. If we regard 666·666 as meaning $600+60+6+\frac{6}{10}+\frac{6}{100}+\frac{6}{1000}$ then the dot, called the decimal point, separates the whole numbers from the fractional parts. Notice that with the fractional, or decimal parts, e.g. ·666, each figure 6 is ten times the value of the following one, reading from left to right. Thus $\frac{6}{10}$ is ten times as great as $\frac{6}{100}$, and $\frac{6}{100}$ is ten times as great as $\frac{6}{1000}$ and so on.

Decimals then are fractions which have denominators of 10, 100, 1000 and so on, according to the position of the figure after the decimal point.

If we have to write six hundred and five we write 605; the zero keeps the place for the missing tens. In the same way if we want to write $\frac{3}{10}+\frac{5}{1000}$ we write ·305; the zero keeps the place for the missing hundredths. Also $\frac{6}{100}+\frac{7}{1000}$ would be written ·067; the zero in this case keeps the place for the missing tenths.

When there are no whole numbers it is usual to insert a zero in front of the decimal point so that, for instance, ·35 would be written 0·35.

Exercise 22

Read off as decimals:

1) $\frac{7}{10}$

2) $\frac{3}{10}+\frac{7}{100}$

3) $\frac{5}{10}+\frac{8}{100}+\frac{9}{1000}$

4) $\frac{9}{1000}$

5) $\frac{3}{100}$

6) $\frac{1}{100}+\frac{7}{1000}$

7) $8+\frac{6}{100}$

8) $24+\frac{2}{100}+\frac{9}{10\,000}$

9) $50+\frac{8}{1000}$

Read off the following with denominators 10, 100, 1000, etc.

10) 0·2
11) 4·6
12) 3·58
13) 437·25
14) 0·004
15) 0·036
16) 400·029
17) 0·001
18) 0·0329

Addition and Subtraction of Decimals

Adding or subtracting decimals is done in exactly the same way as for whole numbers. Care must be taken, however, to write the decimal points directly underneath one another. This makes sure that all the figures having the same place value fall in the same column.

Example 1   Simplify 11·36+2·639+0·047.

$$\begin{array}{r} 11\cdot36 \\ 2\cdot639 \\ 0\cdot047 \\ \hline 14\cdot046 \end{array}$$

Example 2   Subtract 8·567 from 19·126.

$$\begin{array}{r} 19\cdot126 \\ 8\cdot567 \\ \hline 10\cdot559 \end{array}$$

Exercise 23

Write down the values of:

1) 2·375+0·625
2) 4·25+7·25
3) 3·196+2·475+18·369
4) 38·267+0·049+20·3
5) 27·418+0·967+25+1·467
6) 12·48−8·36
7) 19·215−3·599
8) 2·237−1·898
9) 0·876−0·064
10) 5·48−0·0691

Multiplication and Division of Decimals

Example 3   One of the advantages of decimals is the ease with which they may be multiplied or divided by 10, 100, 1000, etc.

Find the value of 1·4×10.

$$1\cdot4\times10 = 1\times10+0\cdot4\times10 = 10+\frac{4}{10}\times10 = 10+4 = 14$$

Example 4   Find the value of 27·532×10.

$$27\cdot532\times10 = 27\times10+0\cdot5\times10+0\cdot03\times10+0\cdot002\times10$$

$$= 270 + \frac{5}{10} \times 10 + \frac{3}{100} \times 10 + \frac{2}{1000} \times 10$$

$$= 270 + 5 + \frac{3}{10} + \frac{2}{100} = 275 \cdot 32$$

In both of the above examples you will notice that the figures have not been changed by the multiplication; only the *positions* of the figures have been changed. Thus in Example 3, $1 \cdot 4 \times 10 = 14$, that is the decimal point has been moved one place to the right. In Example 4, $27 \cdot 532 \times 10 = 275 \cdot 32$; again the decimal point has been moved one place to the right.

To multiply by 10, then, is the same as shifting the decimal point one place to the right. In the same way to multiply by 100 means shifting the decimal point two places to the right and so on.

Example 5 $17 \cdot 369 \times 100 = 1736 \cdot 9$.

The decimal point has been moved two places to the right.

Example 6 $0 \cdot 07895 \times 1000 = 78 \cdot 95$.

The decimal point has been moved three places to the right.

Exercise 24

Multiply each of the following numbers by 10, 100 and 1000.

1) 4·1
2) 2·42
3) 0·046
4) 0·35
5) 0·1486
6) 0·001 753

Write down the values of:

7) 0·4853 × 100
8) 0·009 × 1000
9) 170·06 × 10
10) 0·563 96 × 10 000

When dividing by 10 the decimal point is moved one place to the left, by 100, two places to the left and so on. Thus:

$$154 \cdot 26 \div 10 = 15 \cdot 426$$

The decimal point has been moved one place to the left.

$$9 \cdot 432 \div 100 = 0 \cdot 094\ 32$$

The decimal point has been moved two places to the left.

$$35 \div 1000 = 0 \cdot 035$$

The decimal point has been moved three places to the left.

In the above examples note carefully that use has been made of zeros following the decimal point to keep the places for the missing tenths.

Exercise 25

Divide each of the following numbers by 10, 100 and 1000.

1) 3·6   2) 64·198   3) 0·07   4) 510·4   5) 0·352

THE DECIMAL SYSTEM

Give the value of:

6) $5 \cdot 4 \div 100$
7) $2 \cdot 05 \div 1000$
8) $0 \cdot 04 \div 10$
9) $0 \cdot 0086 \div 1000$
10) $627 \cdot 428 \div 10\,000$

Long Multiplication

Example 7   Find the value of $36 \cdot 5 \times 3 \cdot 504$

First disregard the decimal points and multiply 365 by 3504

$$
\begin{array}{r}
365 \\
3\,504 \\
\hline
1\,095\,000 \\
182\,500 \\
1\,460 \\
\hline
1\,278\,960 \\
\hline
\end{array}
$$

Now count up the total number of figures following the decimal points in both numbers (i.e. $1+3 = 4$). In the answer to the multiplication (the product), count this total number of figures from the right and insert the decimal point. The product is then $127 \cdot 8960$ or $127 \cdot 896$ since the zero does not mean anything.

Exercise 26

Find the values of the following:

1) $25 \cdot 42 \times 29 \cdot 23$
2) $0 \cdot 3618 \times 2 \cdot 63$
3) $0 \cdot 76 \times 0 \cdot 38$
4) $3 \cdot 025 \times 2 \cdot 45$
5) $0 \cdot 043 \times 0 \cdot 032$

Long Division

Example 8   Find the value of $19 \cdot 24 \div 2 \cdot 6$.

First convert the divisor ($2 \cdot 6$) into a whole number by multiplying it by 10. To compensate multiply the dividend ($19 \cdot 24$) by 10 also so that we now have $192 \cdot 4 \div 26$. Now proceed as in ordinary division.

```
26)192·4(7·4
   182      — this line 26 × 7
   ---
    10 4    — 4 brought down from above. Since 4 lies to the right of
    10 4      the decimal point in the dividend insert a decimal point
    ---       in the answer (the quotient)
    . . .
   ---
```

Notice carefully how the decimal point in the quotient was obtained. The 4 brought down from the dividend lies to the right of the decimal point. Before bringing this down put a decimal point in the quotient immediately following the 7.

The division in this case is exact (i.e. there is no remainder) and the answer is 7·4. Now let us see what happens when there is a remainder.

Example 9 Find the value of 15·187÷3·57.

As before make the divisor into a whole number by multiplying it by 100 so that it becomes 357. To compensate multiply the dividend also by 100 so that it becomes 1518·7. Now divide.

```
357)1518·7(4·25406
     1428          —    this line 357×4
     ────
      907          —    7 brought down from the dividend. Since it
      714                lies to the right of the decimal point insert a
      ───                decimal point in the quotient.
     1930          —    Bring down a zero as all the figures in the
     1785                dividend have been used up.
     ────
     1450
     1428
     ────
      2200         —    Bring down a zero. The divisor will not go into
      2142                220 so place 0 in the quotient and bring down
      ────                another zero.
        58
```

The answer to 5 decimal places is 4·25406. This is not the correct answer because there is a remainder. The division can be continued in the way shown to give as many decimal places as desired, or until there is no remainder.

It is important to realise what is meant by an answer given to so many decimal places. It is the number of figures which follow the decimal point which give the number of decimal places. If the first figure to be discarded is 5 or more then the previous figure is increased by 1. Thus:

85·7684 = 85·8 correct to 1 decimal place
       = 85·77 correct to 2 decimal places
       = 85·768 correct to 3 decimal places

Notice carefully that zeros must be kept:

0·007362 = 0·007 correct to 3 decimal places
        = 0·01 correct to 2 decimal places

7·601 = 7·60 correct to 2 decimal places
     = 7·6 correct to 1 decimal place

If an answer is required correct to 3 decimal places the division should be continued to 4 decimal places and the answer corrected to 3 decimal places.

THE DECIMAL SYSTEM

Exercise 27

Find the value of:
1) $18·89 \div 14·2$ correct to 2 decimal places
2) $0·0396 \div 2·51$ correct to 3 decimal places
3) $7·21 \div 0·038$ correct to 2 decimal places
4) $13·059 \div 3·18$ correct to 4 decimal places
5) $0·1382 \div 0·0032$ correct to 1 decimal place

Significant Figures

Instead of using the number of decimal places to express the accuracy of an answer, significant figures can be used. The number 39·38 is correct to 2 decimal places but it is also correct to 4 significant figures since the number contains four figures. The rules regarding significant figures are as follows:

(i) If the first figure to be discarded is 5 or more the previous figure is increased by 1.

$8·1925 = 8·193$ correct to 4 significant figures
$= 8·19$ correct to 3 significant figures
$= 8·2$ correct to 2 significant figures

(ii) Zeros must be kept to show the position of the decimal point, or to indicate that the zero is a significant figure.

$24\,392 = 24\,390$ correct to 4 significant figures
$= 24\,400$ correct to 3 significant figures

$0·0858 = 0·086$ correct to 2 significant figures

$425·804 = 425·80$ correct to 5 significant figures
$= 426$ correct to 3 significant figures

Exercise 28

Write down the following numbers correct to the number of significant figures stated:

1) 24·865 82   i) to 6   ii) to 4   iii) to 2
2) 0·008 357 1   i) to 4   ii) to 3   iii) to 2
3) 4·978 48   i) to 5   ii) to 3   iii) to 1
4) 21·987 to 2
5) 35·603 to 4
6) 28 387 617   i) to 5   ii) to 2
7) 4·149 76   i) to 5   ii) to 4   iii) to 3
8) 9·2048 to 3

Rough Checks for Calculations

The worst mistake that can be made in a calculation is that of misplacing the decimal point. To place it wrongly, even by one place, makes the answer ten times too large or ten times too small. To prevent this occurring it is always worth while doing a rough check by using approximate numbers. When doing these rough checks always try to select numbers which are easy to multiply or which will cancel.

Examples 10

1) 0.23×0.56.

For a rough check we will take 0.2×0.6
Product roughly $= 0.2 \times 0.6 = 0.12$
Correct product $= 0.1288$

(The rough check shows that the answer is 0·1288 not 1·288 or 0·01288)

2) $173.3 \div 27.8$.

For a rough check we will take $180 \div 30$
Quotient roughly $= 6$
Correct quotient $= 6.23$

(Note the rough check and the correct answer are of the same order)

3) $\dfrac{8 \cdot 198 \times 19 \cdot 56 \times 30 \cdot 82 \times 0 \cdot 198}{6 \cdot 52 \times 3 \cdot 58 \times 0 \cdot 823}$.

Answer roughly $= \dfrac{8 \times 20 \times 30 \times 0 \cdot 2}{6 \times 4 \times 1} = 40$

Correct answer $= 50 \cdot 94$.

(Although there is a big difference between the rough answer and the correct answer, the rough check shows that the answer is 50·94 and not 509·4 or 5·094)

Exercise 29

Find rough checks for the following:

1) $223 \cdot 6 \times 0 \cdot 0048$
2) $32 \cdot 7 \times 0 \cdot 259$
3) $0 \cdot 682 \times 0 \cdot 097 \times 2 \cdot 38$
4) $78 \cdot 41 \div 23 \cdot 78$
5) $0 \cdot 059 \div 0 \cdot 002\,68$
6) $33 \cdot 2 \times 29 \cdot 6 \times 0 \cdot 031$
7) $\dfrac{0 \cdot 728 \times 0 \cdot 006\,25}{0 \cdot 0281}$
8) $\dfrac{27 \cdot 5 \times 30 \cdot 52}{11 \cdot 3 \times 2 \cdot 73}$

Fraction to Decimal Conversion

We found, when doing fractions, that the line separating the numerator and the denominator of a fraction takes the place of a division sign. Thus:

$\dfrac{17}{80}$ is the same as $17 \div 80$

Therefore to convert a fraction into a decimal we divide the denominator into the numerator.

THE DECIMAL SYSTEM

Example 11 Convert $\frac{27}{32}$ to decimals.

$\frac{27}{32} = 27 \div 32$

```
32)27·0(0·84375
   25 6
    1 40
    1 28
      120
       96
      240
      224
      160
      160
      ...
```

Therefore $\frac{27}{32} = 0·843\ 75$

Example 12 Convert $2\frac{9}{16}$ into decimals.

When we have a mixed number to convert into decimals we need only deal with the fractional part. Thus to convert $2\frac{9}{16}$ into decimals we only have to deal with $\frac{9}{16}$.

$\frac{9}{16} = 9 \div 16$

```
16)9·0(0·5625
   8 0
   1 00
     96
     40
     32
     80
     80
     ..
```

The division shows that $\frac{9}{16} = 0·5625$ and hence $2\frac{9}{16} = 2.5625$.

Sometimes a fraction will not divide out exactly as shown in Example 13.

Example 13 Convert $\frac{1}{3}$ to decimals.

$\frac{1}{3} = 1 \div 3$

```
3)1·0(0·333
   9
   10
    9
   10
    9
    1
```

It is clear that all we shall get from the division is a succession of threes.

This is an example of a recurring decimal and in order to prevent endless repetition the result is written 0·3̇. Therefore $\frac{1}{3} = 0·\dot{3}$.

Some further examples of recurring decimals are:

$\frac{2}{3} = 0·\dot{6}$ (meaning 0·6666..... etc.)

$\frac{1}{6} = 0·1\dot{6}$ (meaning 0·1666..... etc.)

$\frac{5}{11} = 0·\dot{4}\dot{5}$ (meaning 0·454545..... etc.)

$\frac{3}{7} = 0·\dot{4}2857\dot{1}$ (meaning 0·428571428571..... etc.)

For all practical purposes we never need recurring decimals; what we need is an answer given to so many significant figures or decimal places. Thus:

$\frac{2}{3} = 0·67$ (correct to 2 decimal places)

$\frac{5}{11} = 0·455$ (correct to 3 significant figures)

Exercise 30

Convert the following to decimals correcting the answers, where necessary, to 4 decimal places:

1) $\frac{1}{4}$
2) $\frac{3}{4}$
3) $\frac{3}{8}$
4) $\frac{11}{16}$
5) $\frac{1}{2}$
6) $\frac{2}{3}$
7) $\frac{21}{32}$
8) $\frac{29}{64}$
9) $1\frac{5}{6}$
10) $2\frac{7}{16}$

Write down the following recurring decimals correct to 3 decimal places:

11) 0·$\dot{3}$
12) 0·$\dot{7}$
13) 0·1$\dot{3}$
14) 0·1$\dot{8}$
15) 0·3$\dot{5}$
16) 0·$\dot{2}\dot{3}$
17) 0·5$\dot{2}$
18) 0·3$\dot{8}$
19) 0·32$\dot{8}$
20) 0·$\dot{5}67\dot{1}$

Conversion of Decimals to Fractions

We know that decimals are fractions with denominators 10, 100, 1000 etc. Using this fact we can always convert a decimal to a fraction.

Example 14 Convert 0·32 to a fraction.

$$0·32 = \frac{32}{100} = \frac{8}{25}$$

When comparing decimals and fractions it is best to convert the fraction into a decimal.

THE DECIMAL SYSTEM

Example 15 Find the difference between $1\frac{3}{16}$ and $1\cdot1632$.

$$1\frac{3}{16} = 1\cdot1875$$

$$1\frac{3}{16} - 1\cdot1632 = 1\cdot1875 - 1\cdot1632 = 0\cdot0243$$

Exercise 31

Convert the following to fractions in their lowest terms:

1) 0·2
2) 0·45
3) 0·3125
4) 2·55
5) 0·0075
6) 2·125
7) What is the difference between 0·28135 and $\frac{9}{32}$?
8) What is the difference between $\frac{19}{64}$ and 0·295?

Summary

1) Decimals are fractions with denominators of 10, 100, 1000 etc. The decimal point separates the whole numbers from the fractional parts.
2) When adding or subtracting decimal numbers the decimal points are written under one another.
3) To multiply by 10 move the decimal point one place to the right, to multiply by 100 move the decimal point two places to the right, etc.
4) To divide by 10 move the decimal point one place to the left, to divide by 100 move the decimal point two places to the left, etc.
5) When multiplying first disregard the decimal points and multiply the two numbers as though they were whole numbers. To place the decimal point in the product, count up the total number of figures after the decimal point in both numbers and then in the product count this number of figures starting from the extreme right.
6) When dividing first make the divisor into a whole number and compensate the dividend.
7) Significant figures and decimal places are used to denote the accuracy of a number.
8) Before multiplying or dividing always perform a rough check which will ensure that the decimal point is placed correctly.
9) To convert a fraction into a decimal divide the numerator by the denominator.
10) When comparing fractions and decimals, convert the fraction into a decimal.

Mental Test 3

Try to write down the answers to the following without writing anything else.

1) Add 1·2, 1·3 and 2·5.
2) Add 0·21, 0·32, 0·73 and 0·51.
3) Add 1·01, 1·20, 31 and 0·20.
4) Subtract 0·64 from 1·86.
5) Take 1·04 from 3·16.
6) Take 3·98 from 4·06.
7) Multiply 2·3 by 5.
8) Multiply 0·83 by 7.
9) Multiply 1·43 by 4.
10) Multiply 0·06 by 8.
11) Multiply 1·03 by 9.
12) Divide 0·84 by 7.
13) Divide 1·35 by 9.
14) Divide 19·2 by 8.
15) Divide 0·091 by 0·07.

Self-Test 3

In questions 1 to 10 state the letter, or letters, corresponding to the correct answer or answers.

1) The number 0·028 57 correct to 3 places of decimals is
   a 0·028 **b** 0·029 **c** 0·286 **d** 0·0286

2) The sum of $5 + \frac{1}{100} + \frac{7}{1000}$ is
   a 5·17 **b** 5·017 **c** 5·0107 **d** 5·107

3) 13·0063 × 1000 is equal to
   a 13·063   **b** 1300·63
   c 130·063   **d** 13 006·3

4) 1·5003 ÷ 100 is equal to
   a 0·015 003   **b** 0·150 03
   c 0·153   **d** 1·53

5) 18·2 × 0·013 × 5·21 is equal to
   a 12·326 86   **b** 123·2686
   c 1·232 686   **d** 0·123 268 6

6) The number 158 861 correct to 2 significant figures is
   a 15   **b** 150 000
   c 16   **d** 160 000

7) The number 0·081 778 correct to 3 significant figures is
   a 0·082 **b** 0·081 **c** 0·0818 **d** 0·0817

8) The number 0·075 538 correct to 2 decimal places is
   a 0·076 **b** 0·075 **c** 0·07 **d** 0·08

9) The number 0·1 $\dot{6}$ correct to 4 significant figures is
   a 0·1616 **b** 0·1617 **c** 0.1667 **d** 0·1666

10) 0·017 ÷ 0·027 is equal to (correct to 2 significant figures)
   a 0·63 **b** 6·3 **c** 0·063 **d** 63

In questions 11 to 20 the answer is either true or false. State which.

11) $\frac{5}{100} + \frac{5}{10000} = 0 \cdot 0505$

12) $5 + \frac{1}{10} + \frac{3}{1000} = 5 \cdot 13$

13) 8·26 − 1·38 − 2·44 = 4·44

14) 11·011 × 100 = 1111

15) 0·101 01 ÷ 100 = 0·010 101

16) $0 \cdot 0302 = \frac{3}{100} + \frac{2}{1000}$

17) 20 963 = 21 000, correct to 2 significant figures

18) 0·099 83 = 0·10, correct to 2 significant figures

19) 0·007 891 = 0·008, correct to 3 decimal places

20) 0·5 ÷ 0·2 = 2·5

4. Money and Simple Accounts

UNDERSTAND THE METRIC SYSTEM OF UNITS AS CURRENTLY IN USE IN BUSINESS

Perform business calculations involving currency, length, weight and capacity.

The British System

The British system of decimal currency uses the pound as the basic unit. The only sub-unit used is the penny such that:

100 pence = 1 pound

The abbreviation p is used for pence and the abbreviation £ is used for pounds. A decimal point is used to separate the pounds from the pence, for example:

£3·58 meaning three pounds and fifty-eight pence

There are two ways of expressing amounts less than £1. For example 74 pence may be written as £0·74 or 74 p; 5 pence may be written as £0·05 or as 5 p.

The smallest unit used is the half-penny which is always written as a fraction i.e. as $\frac{1}{2}$. Thus £5·17$\frac{1}{2}$ means 5 pounds and 17$\frac{1}{2}$ pence. 53$\frac{1}{2}$ pence is written as either 53$\frac{1}{2}$ p or as £0·53$\frac{1}{2}$. Note carefully that $\frac{1}{2}$ p = £0·005, a fact which is useful when solving some problems with decimal currency.

Addition and Subtraction

The addition of sums of money is done in almost the same way as the addition of decimals. The exception occurs with the half-pence piece.

Example 1 Add together £3·78, £5·23 and £8·19.

£3·78
£5·23
£8·19
———
£17·20

Write down the amounts with the decimal points directly beneath one another. First add the pence which total 120. This is equal to £1·20 so we write 20 in the pence columns and carry the £1. Now add the pounds $1+8+5+3 = 17$.

Example 2 Add together £2·58$\frac{1}{2}$, £3·27$\frac{1}{2}$ and £5·73$\frac{1}{2}$.

£2·58$\frac{1}{2}$
£3·27$\frac{1}{2}$
£5·73$\frac{1}{2}$
———
£11·59$\frac{1}{2}$

First add the half-pence and we get 1$\frac{1}{2}$ p. Write $\frac{1}{2}$ in the answer and carry 1 p. Now add the whole pence: $1+73+27+58 = 159$ p. This is equal to £1·59 so write 59 in the answer and carry £1. Finally add the pounds thus: $1+2+3+5 = £11$.

Example 3   Add together 39 p, $84\frac{1}{2}$ p and £1·73.

£0·39   When amounts are given in pence it is best to write these as
£0·84$\frac{1}{2}$ pounds. Thus 39 p is written £0·39, etc. The addition is
£1·73   then performed as previously described.
─────
£2·96$\frac{1}{2}$

Example 4   Subtract £2·36$\frac{1}{2}$ from £3·08.

£3·08   We cannot take $36\frac{1}{2}$ p from 8 p so we borrow £1 = 100 p
£2·36$\frac{1}{2}$ from the £3 on the top line. Then $108 - 36\frac{1}{2} = 71\frac{1}{2}$. The £3
─────   becomes £2 and we have $2 - 2 = 0$ thus giving an answer of
£0·71$\frac{1}{2}$ £0·71$\frac{1}{2}$ or $71\frac{1}{2}$ p

Exercise 32

1) Express the following amounts as pence: £0·68, £0·63, £0·58$\frac{1}{2}$.

2) Express the following as pence: £2·16, £3·59$\frac{1}{2}$, £17·68.

3) Express the following as pounds: 35 p, 78$\frac{1}{2}$ p, 6 p, 3 p.

4) Express the following as pounds: 246 p, 983$\frac{1}{2}$ p, 26 532 p.

5) Add the following sums of money together:
  (a) £2·15, £3·28, £4·63
  (b) £8·28, £109·17, £27·98, £70·15
  (c) £0·17$\frac{1}{2}$, £1·63$\frac{1}{2}$, £1·71, £1·90$\frac{1}{2}$
  (d) 82 p, 71 p, 82 p
  (e) 17$\frac{1}{2}$ p, 27 p, 81$\frac{1}{2}$ p, 74$\frac{1}{2}$ p

6) Subtract the following:
  (a) £7·60 from £9·84
  (b) £3·49 from £11·42
  (c) £18·73$\frac{1}{2}$ from £87·35
  (d) £0·54$\frac{1}{2}$ from £1·32$\frac{1}{2}$
  (e) 54 p from £2·63$\frac{1}{2}$

Balancing

When dealing with the addition and subtraction of sums of money it is impossible to be too careful. Whenever possible checks should be made and one way of doing this is the method of balancing.

Example 5   The following table shows the amounts of money taken by various departments of a large store during six successive weeks.

	Grocery	Toys	Childs wear	Womens wear	Mens wear
Week 1	£2087·58	£976·43	£875·34	£1794·69	£1068·89
Week 2	£2165·42	£758·58	£918·89	£1689·73	£1265·98
Week 3	£2200·31	£834·67	£812·89	£2178·98	£1358·90
Week 4	£2178·95	£768·50	£805·12	£2334·42	£1234·56
Week 5	£2317·78	£812·34	£798·03	£3217·87	£1178·92
Week 6	£2412·67	£913·42	£821·76	£2816·33	£1245·89

Add separately each column and each row and check by obtaining the overall totals for each.

MONEY AND SIMPLE ACCOUNTS 37

	Grocery	Toys	Childs wear	Womens wear	Mens wear	Totals
Week 1	£2087·58	£976·43	£875·34	£1794·69	£1068·89	£6802·93
Week 2	£2165·42	£758·58	£918·89	£1689·73	£1265·98	£6798·60
Week 3	£2200·31	£834·67	£812·89	£2178·98	£1358·90	£7385·75
Week 4	£2178·95	£768·50	£805·12	£2334·42	£1234·56	£7321·55
Week 5	£2317·78	£812·34	£798·03	£3217·87	£1178·92	£8324·94
Week 6	£2412·67	£913·42	£821·76	£2816·33	£1245·89	£8210·07
Totals	£13 362·71	£5063·94	£5032·03	£14 032·02	£7353·14	£44 843·84

The overall total is shown within the box. All the additions are correct if the overall total obtained by adding the vertical total column equals the overall total obtained by adding the horizontal total row.

Exercise 33

1) The table below shows the weekly expenditure of a household for four successive weeks. Find the total expenditure for each week and also the total expenditure for each item for the four weeks. Finally add together the vertical and horizontal totals to obtain the final total for the four weeks.

	Food	Clothing	Heating	Rent	Sundries	Totals
Week 1	£26·70	£9·48	£9·60	£18·00	£4·05	
Week 2	£23·55	£7·59	£12·48	£18·00	£2·34	
Week 3	£28·08	£14·94	£11·34	£18·00	£1·68	
Week 4	£25·89	£6·39	£15·18	£18·00	£3.75	
Totals						

2) The following table shows the earnings of 5 men during the month of July. Work out the vertical and horizontal totals as shown and by finding the overall total perform a balance.

	Man A	Man B	Man C	Man D	Man E	Totals
Week 1	£91·52	£79·76	£103·26	£175·24	£99·76	
Week 2	£85·78	£87·34	£109·36	£157·80	£102·54	
Week 3	£105·56	£129·36	£106·44	£161·62	£97·38	
Week 4	£155·66	£99·46	£100·00	£142·84	£72·50	
Totals						

3) The table overleaf shows income tax deductions made from a woman's earnings during six months of a tax year. Calculate the weekly and monthly totals and perform a balance.

	Week 1	Week 2	Week 3	Week 4	Week 5	Totals
April	—	£4·75	£4·28	£3·98	—	
May	£4·03	£4·16	£4·08	£4·27	—	
June	£3·79	£3·89	£4·33	£3·78	—	
July	£4·16	£4·12	£4·13	£4·33	£3·88	
August	£3·77	£6·23	£4·08	£3·77	—	
September	£3·99	£4·43	£4·00	£3·79	—	
Totals						

Financial Statements

It is important that you should be able to understand a financial statement. The one which is shown below is a statement for a Club Dance.

Income — *Expenditure*

Date	Particulars	Receipts	Date	Particulars	Payments
8/6	Sale of 400 tickets @ £2	800·00	11/6	Hire of hall	75·00
			17/6	Printing of tickets	33·50
20/6	Sale of 250 tickets @ £2	500·00	23/6	Cost of band	180·00
23/6	Sale of tickets at door. 120 @ £2·50	300·00	23/6	Cost of buffet @ £1 per head	770·00
					1058·50
				Balance carried down	541·50
	Total	£1600·00			£1600·00

The statement shows clearly how much money has been received and how much has been spent. The balance carried down is the profit made on the dance and it is found by subtracting the total payments (£1058·50) from the total receipts (£1600·00). This balance is added to the total payments and both sides of the book i.e. income and expenditure should be the same.

The accounts for business transactions are kept in a book called the ledger which is usually ruled as shown in Example 6. The general rule for entering up ledger accounts is:

debit—the amounts of money placed in the account
credit—the amounts of money flowing out of the account

Example 6 Enter the following transactions in a Cash Account. Balance the account and bring down the balance.

1/5 Cash in hand £58·73
8/5 Paid telephone bill £33·40
10/5 Received cash from L. Thomas £29·00
12/5 Bought goods for cash £15·74
15/5 Cash sales £89·70
18/5 Paid into bank £75·00

MONEY AND SIMPLE ACCOUNTS

Dr			Cash a/c			Cr
		£				£
May 1	To balance b/d	58·73	May 8	By telephone		33·40
May 10	,, L. Thomas	29·00	May 12	,, purchases		15·74
May 15	,, sales	89·70	May 18	,, bank		75·00
		177·43	May 20	,, balance c/d		53·29
May 22	To balance	53·29				177·43

The following points should be carefully noted:

(1) The name of the account is Cash a/c (a/c stands for account).
(2) Left hand side: Dr = debit. Right hand side: Cr = credit.
(3) c/d stands for carried down. b/d stands for brought down.
(4) For the entries receipts are entered under Dr and payments are entered under Cr.
(5) On the debit side all entries are prefixed 'to' and the name of the account from which the money is received is stated.
(6) On the credit side all entries are prefixed 'by' and the name of the account into which the money is paid is stated.
(7) The opening balance is the amount left in the account from the previous period.
(8) The closing balance is the amount necessary for the account to balance. On the credit side the payments made amount to £33·40 + £15·74 + £75·00 = £124·14. The closing balance is found by subtracting this from the total receipts of £177·43 giving a closing balance of £53·29. Thus the account shows that we have a balance of £53·29 in our cash account on May 22nd.

Exercise 34

Draw up financial statements to show the following transactions taking care to balance the receipts and payments columns.

1) Hockey club accounts:

    1/9 Annual subscriptions 32 members @ £4.50 each
    10/9 Match fees for game v Old Manorians £16·50
    10/9 Cost of teas for game v Old Manorians £12·60
    10/9 Umpires expenses £2·25
    17/9 Match fees for mixed game v Moorpark £12·60
    17/9 Cost of teas £13·80
    17/9 Umpires expenses £1.65

2) Annual outing of Youth Club:

    5/7 Received £2·40 from each of 70 members
    7/7 Received subsidy of £75 from General Committee
    9/7 Hire of 2 coaches and drivers £108
    9/7 Cost of 72 teas at £1·80 each

3) Firm's annual sports day:

    3/6 Received subsidy from directors £100
    5/6 Received £62 from competitors
    8/6 Hire of tents £116
    8/6 Competitors prizes £216
    8/6 Cost of raffle tickets and prizes £25·80
    8/6 Sale of raffle tickets £81·90

4) Enter the following transactions in the Cash account. Balance the account and bring down the balance.

    1st Jan Cash in hand £39·47
    5th Jan Paid telephone account £17·89
    8th Jan Received cash from P. Smith £42·00
    12th Jan Bought goods for cash £53·25
    29th Jan Cash sales £108·75
    31st Jan Paid into bank £105·00

5) Enter the following transactions in a Cash account. Balance the account and bring down the balance.

    3rd March Cash in hand £97·57
    9th March Bought goods for cash £73·78
    16th March Cash sales £128·97
    18th March Received from T. Barnes £54·00
    28th March Banked £175·00
    30th March Bought postage stamps £3·40

Petty Cash Book

Most offices keep a small amount of cash available for day to day running expenses such as cost of postage stamps, stationery, etc. This cash is called petty cash and it is important that an account be kept of how the money is spent. The account is kept in the petty cash book and it is prepared in much the same way as the financial statements previously discussed.

Example 7   Enter the following transactions in a petty cash book.

    1st Jan Petty cash in hand £24·00
    3rd Jan Parcel post £2·25
    4th Jan Letter postage £2·52
    5th Jan Window cleaner £3·60
    6th Jan Purchase of stationery £4·05
    7th Jan Received reimbursement for the week's expenditure to keep balance in hand at £24·00

Receipts	Date	Particulars	Payments
24·00	1st Jan	Cash in hand	
	3rd Jan	Parcel post	2·25
	4th Jan	Letter Post	2·52
	5th Jan	Window cleaner	3·60
	6th Jan	Stationery	4·05
		Total	12·42
12·42	7th Jan	Reimbursement	
		Balance carried down	24·00
36·42			36·42

Sometimes it is desirable to know how much petty cash has been spent on the various items for a given period. For instance we might want to know how much has been spent on postage or on cleaning, etc. The method of entering the items shown in Example 7 is not very satisfactory in this respect because to obtain the information required

MONEY AND SIMPLE ACCOUNTS   41

                    means adding together several different entries. It is therefore better to set out the petty cash book in analysis columns as shown in Example 8.

Example 8   A petty cash book has analysis columns for postage, stationery, travelling expenses, office expenses and cleaning. Enter the following transactions:

        2nd July Received from cashier £30
        3rd July Bus fare 84p, postage £1.47
        4th July Envelopes £1·95, string 72p
        5th July Parcel post £2·28, office tea £2·10
        6th July Window cleaning, £6·90, railway fares £3·75
        7th July Pencils £1·20, cleaners wages £7·50
        9th July Received reimbursement for the week's expenditure to keep balance in hand at £30

Receipts	Date	Particulars	Payments	Postage	Stationery	Travelling Expenses	Office Expenses	Cleaning
30·00	2nd July	Balance in hand						
	3rd July	Bus fare	0·84			0·84		
	3rd July	Postage	1·47	1·47				
	4th July	Envelopes	1·95		1·95			
	4th July	String	0·72		0·72			
	5th July	Parcel post	2·28	2·28				
	5th July	Office tea	2·10				2·10	
	6th July	Window cleaning	6·90					6·90
	6th July	Railway fares	3·75			3·75		
	7th July	Pencils	1·20		1·20			
	7th July	Cleaners wages	7·50					7·50
		Totals	28·71	3·75	3·87	4·59	2·10	14·40
28·71	9th July	Reimbursement						
		Balance carried down	30·00					
58·71			58·71					

Exercise 35

1) Enter the following transactions in a suitably ruled petty cash book:

    8th Jan Petty cash balance in hand £27.00
    9th Jan Postage £2·28
    10th Jan Parcel post £2·79, window cleaner £3, bus fares 96p
    11th Jan Ball point pens £1·05, envelopes £1.92, Xerox copying 96p
    12th Jan Taxi fare £2·61, string 84p
    13th Jan Cleaners wages £9
    15th Jan Reimbursement to keep balance in hand at £27

2) Enter the following transactions in a petty cash book which has analysis columns for postage, stationery, travelling expenses, cleaning and office expenses:

   3rd Jan Petty cash balance in hand £36
   4th Jan Postage £2·82, Xerox copying £1·92
   5th Jan Pencils £1·44, train fare £2·34, office tea £2·04
   6th Jan Window cleaning £4·05, typewriter ribbons £2·25
   7th Jan Parcel postage £2·61, note-paper £2·40
   8th Jan Office tea £2·25, cleaners wages £10·50
  10th Jan Reimbursement to keep cash in hand at £36

3) Enter the following transactions in a petty cash book which has three analysis columns for postage, stationery and travelling expenses.

   5th June Balance in hand £48, postage stamps £6
   6th June Envelopes £1·89, bus fares 84p
   7th June Note-paper £1·35, parcel post £2·94
   8th June Erasers £1·05, railway fares £1·38, pencils £1·35
   9th June Envelopes £1·62, string £1·08
  12th June Reimbursement to keep cash in hand (or *float*) at £48

Multiplication and Division

The multiplication and division of decimal currency are very similar to the methods used with decimal numbers.

Example 9   Find the cost of 23 articles if each costs 27p.

    Now 27p = £0·27

    Cost of 23 articles @ £0·27 = 23 × £0·27 = £6·21

Example 10   Find the cost of 19 articles costing $21\frac{1}{2}$ p each.

    Now $21\frac{1}{2}$ p = £0·215

    Cost of 19 articles @ £0·215 each = £$4·08\frac{1}{2}$

    (Note that $\frac{1}{2}$ p = £0·005 and hence £4·085 = £$4·08\frac{1}{2}$)

Example 11   If 127 articles cost £$14·60\frac{1}{2}$ find the cost of each article.

    Now £$14·60\frac{1}{2}$ is a mixture of decimals and fractions and the first step is to make it into a wholly decimal number by remembering that $\frac{1}{2}$ p = £0·005. Hence:

    £$14·60\frac{1}{2}$ = £14·605.

    £14·605 ÷ 127 = £$0·11\frac{1}{2}$ or $11\frac{1}{2}$ p

Exercise 36

1) Find the cost of 12 articles costing 15p each.

2) Find the cost of 85 articles costing $7\frac{1}{2}$ p each.

MONEY AND SIMPLE ACCOUNTS

3) How much does 43 articles @ $39\frac{1}{2}$ p each cost?

4) What is the cost of 24 articles costing $£7·03\frac{1}{2}$ each?

5) If 12 identical articles cost £1·56, how much does each cost?

6) If 241 identical articles cost $£51·81\frac{1}{2}$, how much does each cost?

7) If 5000 articles cost £6525, find the cost of each article.

8) If 125 articles cost $£270·62\frac{1}{2}$, what is the cost of each article?

Invoices

An invoice is a record of the goods supplied by a manufacturer or wholesaler to a retailer. It looks rather like a bill but it is not a demand for payment. A copy of the invoice is usually sent by post to the purchaser when the goods are dispatched. At this stage only simple invoices are discussed; no attempt is made to deal with discounts etc., and the discount arrangements have been left out on the typical sample invoice shown below.

and the discount arrangements have been left out on the typical sample invoice shown below.

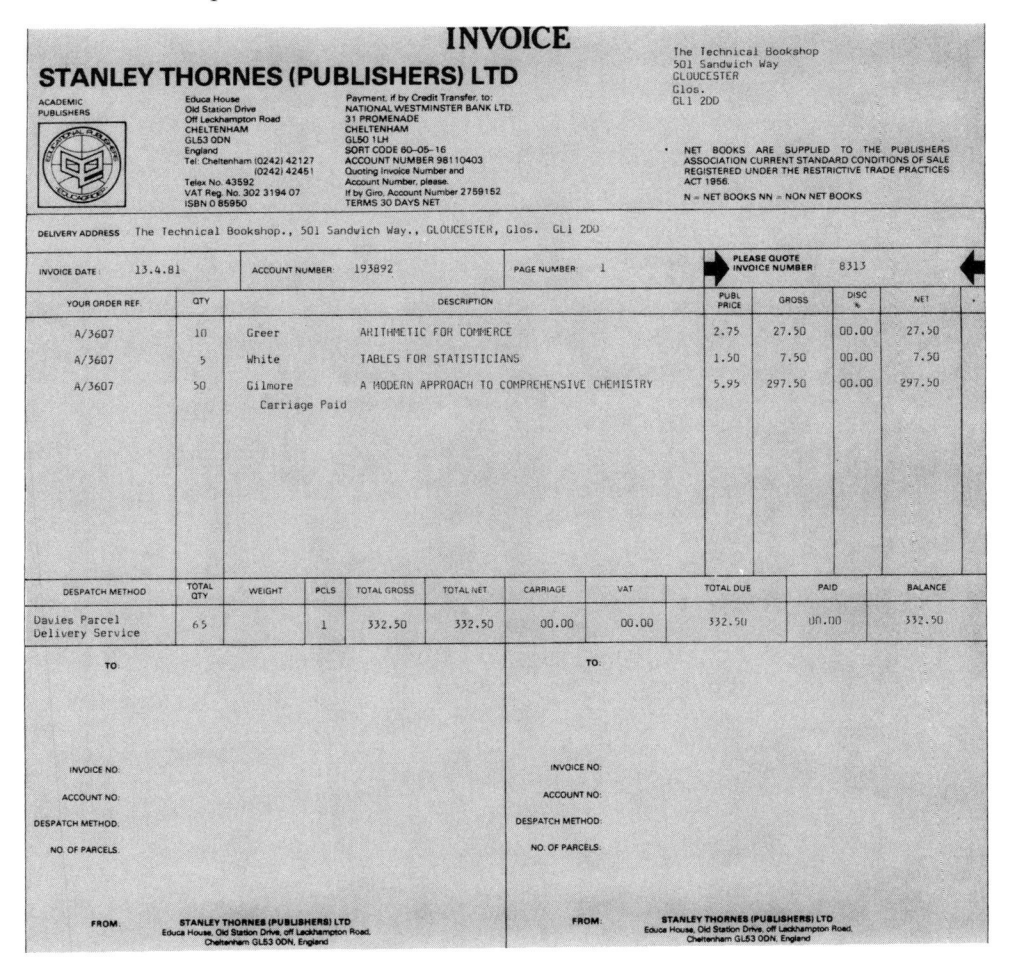

YOUR ORDER REF.	QTY	DESCRIPTION		PUBL PRICE	GROSS	DISC %	NET
A/3607	10	Greer	ARITHMETIC FOR COMMERCE	2.75	27.50	00.00	27.50
A/3607	5	White	TABLES FOR STATISTICIANS	1.50	7.50	00.00	7.50
A/3607	50	Gilmore	A MODERN APPROACH TO COMPREHENSIVE CHEMISTRY	5.95	297.50	00.00	297.50
		Carriage Paid					

Invoice No. 8313, Invoice Date 13.4.81, Account Number 193892, Page Number 1

Despatch Method: Davies Parcel Delivery Service, Total Qty 65, PCLS 1, Total Gross 332.50, Total Net 332.50, Carriage 00.00, VAT 00.00, Total Due 332.50, Paid 00.00, Balance 332.50

STANLEY THORNES (PUBLISHERS) LTD

The last column is found by multiplying the quantity by the unit price. The total amount owed by the purchaser is £332·50, which is the total of the last column.

Exercise 37

Complete the following invoices:
1)

Quantity	Description	Unit cost	£
10	Single sheets	£6·75	
25	Double sheets	£12·15	
20	Bedspreads	£23·85	
5	Quilts	£38·40	

2)

Quantity	Description	Unit cost	£
20	Bath towels	£6·20	
15	Hand towels	£2·10	
30	Small towels	£1·36	
50	Flannels	£0·25	

Make out invoices for the following goods:

3) 50 m of rayon taffeta at £1·75½ per metre
   40 m nylon taffeta at £4·59 per metre
   35 m of rayon brocade at £4·41 per metre
   30 m nylon chiffon at £4·68 per metre

4) 4 bookshelves at £13·48 each
   5 wardrobes at £47·30 each
   6 beds at £39·55 each
   10 sideboards at £52·50 each
   20 dining room chairs at £15·45 each

5) 10 dolls at £1·98 each
   20 dolls' dresses at 45 p each
   5 dolls' prams at £12·35 each
   3 dolls' cots at £7·48 each
   4 dolls' beds at £3·48 each

Mental Test 4

Try to answer the following questions without writing anything down except the answer.

1) Add £1·36, £2·33 and £3·54.
2) Find the cost of 10 articles if they cost 6 p each.
3) Find the cost of 100 articles if they cost £1·20 each.
4) Find the cost of one article if 10 cost 75 p.
5) 100 similar articles cost £1·50. How much does each cost?
6) Find the cost of 20 articles at 15 p each.
7) 25 articles cost £5. How much does each cost?
8) Find the cost of 5 articles at 99 p each.
9) Find the cost of 8 articles at 99 p each.
10) Find the cost of 50 articles at 30 p each.

Self-Test 4

In the following questions decide if the given answer is true or false.

1) In the British system of decimal currency, 100 p = £1.
2) £1·78 means one pound and 78 pence.
3) 36 pence may be written as £.36.
4) One half-penny is equal to £0·005.
5) $58\frac{1}{2}$ p + 27 p is equal to £0·85$\frac{1}{2}$.
6) $73\frac{1}{2}$ p may be written as £0·735.
7) The cost of 5 articles each costing $7\frac{1}{2}$ p is £0·37$\frac{1}{2}$.
8) If 10 articles cost £3·75 the cost of each article is $37\frac{1}{2}$ p.
9) If 25 articles cost £19 each article costs £0·76.
10) Sheets cost £2·75 each. The cost of 20 sheets is £55.

5. The Metric System

UNDERSTAND THE METRIC (AND IMPERIAL SYSTEM) OF UNITS AS CURRENTLY IN USE IN BUSINESS

Convert units within the metric system.

Introduction

In this chapter we shall first deal with the metric system as applied to mass, length and capacity. Then the addition, subtraction, multiplication and division of metric quantities are discussed. Finally domestic problems involving the metric system are discussed.

The Metric System for Length

The metric system is essentially a decimal system. The standard unit of length is the metre but for some purposes the metre is too large a unit and it is therefore split up into smaller units as follows:

$$1 \text{ metre (m)} = 10 \text{ decimetres (dm)}$$
$$= 100 \text{ centimetres (cm)}$$
$$= 1000 \text{ millimetres (mm)}$$

When dealing with large distances the metre is too small a unit and large distances are measured in kilometres.

$$1 \text{ kilometre (km)} = 1000 \text{ metres}$$

Since the metric system is essentially a decimal system we can easily convert from one unit to another by simply moving the decimal point the required number of places.

Example 1 Convert 3·792 m into centimetres.

$$1 \text{ m} = 100 \text{ cm}$$
$$3 \cdot 792 \text{ m} = 100 \times 3 \cdot 792 \text{ cm} = 379 \cdot 2 \text{ cm}$$

Example 2 Convert 98 375 mm into metres.

$$1000 \text{ mm} = 1 \text{ m}$$
$$1 \text{ mm} = \frac{1}{1000} \text{ m}$$
$$98\,375 \text{ mm} = \frac{98\,375}{1000} \text{ m} = 98 \cdot 375 \text{ m}$$

Sometimes you may have difficulty in deciding whether to multiply or divide when converting from one unit to another. If you remember that when converting to a smaller unit you multiply and when converting to a larger unit you divide, this difficulty will disappear.

The Metric System for Mass

The standard unit of mass is the kilogram which is suitable for most purposes connected with weights and measures. However for some purposes the kilogram is too large a unit and the gram is then used. For very small masses the milligram is used. For very large masses the tonne is used.

$$1 \text{ tonne (t)} = 1000 \text{ kilograms (kg)}$$
$$1 \text{ kilogram (kg)} = 1000 \text{ grams (g)}$$
$$1 \text{ gram} = 1000 \text{ milligrams (mg)}$$

Example 3   Convert 5397 mg into grams

$$1000 \text{ mg} = 1 \text{ g}$$
$$1 \text{ mg} = \frac{1}{1000} \text{ g}$$
$$5397 \text{ mg} = \frac{5397}{1000} \text{ g} = 5.397 \text{ g}$$

Example 4   Convert 2·56 kg into grams.

$$1 \text{ kg} = 1000 \text{ g}$$
$$2.56 \text{ kg} = 1000 \times 2.56 \text{ g} = 2560 \text{ g}$$

Capacity

Quantities of liquid are usually measured in litres (ℓ). Small quantities are often measured in millilitres (mℓ) such that:
$$1 \ell = 1000 \text{ m}\ell$$

Example 5   Convert 562 mℓ into litres.

$$562 \text{ m}\ell = \frac{562}{1000} = 0.562 \ell$$

Example 6   A medicine bottle holds 0·65 ℓ. How many 5 mℓ doses can be obtained?

$$1 \ell = 1000 \text{ m}\ell$$
$$0.65 \ell = 0.65 \times 1000 = 650 \text{ m}\ell$$
$$\text{Number of 5 m}\ell \text{ doses} = \frac{650}{5} = 130$$

Exercise 38

1) Convert to metres:
  (a) 5·63 km   (b) 0·68 km
  (c) 17·698 km   (d) 592 cm
  (e) 68 cm   (f) 6895 mm
  (g) 73 mm   (h) 4597 cm
  (i) 798 mm   (j) 5 mm

2) Convert to kilometres:
  (a) 9753 m   (b) 259 m
  (c) 58 m   (d) 2985 cm
  (e) 790 685 mm

THE METRIC SYSTEM

3) Convert to centimetres:
   (a) 4·68 m   (b) 0·782 m
   (c) 5·16 km   (d) 3897 mm
   (e) 88 mm

4) Convert to millimetres:
   (a) 1·234 m   (b) 0·58 km
   (c) 25·8 cm   (d) 389 cm
   (e) 0·052 m

5) Convert to kilograms:
   (a) 530 g   (b) 35 000 g
   (c) 2473 mg   (d) 597 600 mg
   (e) 58 t   (f) 127 t

6) Convert into grams:
   (a) 56 000 mg   (b) 96 mg
   (c) 8·63 kg   (d) 0·081 kg
   (e) 584 mg

7) (a) Convert to litres:
      (i) 450 mℓ (ii) 8762 mℓ
   (b) Convert to millilitres:
      (i) 2·65 ℓ (ii) 0·632 ℓ

8) A wine bottle holds $1\frac{1}{2}$ litres. How many full glasses each containing 32 mℓ can be obtained from the bottle?

The Addition and Subtraction of Metric Quantities

When adding or subtracting lengths or masses it is important that all the quantities be converted to a common unit.

Example 7   Add together 36·1 m, 39·2 cm and 532 mm and express the answer in metres.

$$39\cdot 2 \text{ cm} = \frac{39\cdot 2}{100} \text{ m} = 0\cdot 392 \text{ m}$$

$$532 \text{ mm} = \frac{532}{1000} \text{ m} = 0\cdot 532 \text{ m}$$

We now have to add the lengths 36·1 m, 0·392 m and 0·532 m. We write the numbers down in the same way as when adding decimal numbers, that is, with the decimal points directly underneath each other. Thus

$$\begin{array}{r} 36\cdot 1 \\ 0\cdot 392 \\ 0\cdot 532 \\ \hline 37\cdot 024 \\ \hline \end{array}$$

The answer is therefore, 37·024 m.

Example 8   From a length of cloth 120 m long, the following lengths are cut: $3\frac{1}{2}$ m, $30\frac{1}{4}$ m, 18 m 36 cm and 8 m 27 cm. What length of cloth remains?

Converting all the lengths to metres and decimals of a metre we have:

   Lengths cut off = 3·5 m, 30·25 m, 18·36 m and 8·27 m
   Adding these lengths together

$$\begin{array}{r} 3\cdot 5 \\ 30\cdot 25 \\ 18\cdot 36 \\ 8\cdot 27 \\ \hline 60\cdot 38 \\ \hline \end{array}$$

Hence the total length cut off the cloth is 60·38 m. To find the length remaining we have to subtract 60·38 m from 120 m. Thus

```
120·00
 60·38
------
 59·62
```

Hence 59·62 m of cloth remains.

Exercise 39

1) Add together 39 cm, 3·62 m and 497 mm and express the answer in millimetres.

2) Add together 26·3 cm, 347 mm and 0·783 m and express the answer in metres.

3) A piece of cord 1·3 m long has the following lengths cut from it: 26 cm, $\frac{1}{2}$ m, 358 mm and 12 cm. How much cord remains?

4) Add together the following masses and express the answer in kilograms: 583 g, 19·164 kg and 20 500 mg.

5) A housewife buys the following items of food: 500 g tomatoes, 3 kg potatoes, 250 g butter and $\frac{1}{2}$ kg of sugar. What is the total mass of her purchases?

6) A greengrocer starts the day with 85 kg of apples. He sells $2\frac{1}{2}$ kg, 500 g, 2500 g, $3\frac{1}{4}$ kg and 2 kg 250 g. What mass of apples has he left?

7) A motorist drives 5·8 km to work, but on the way he has to make a detour of 750 m. He drives to a hotel for lunch which is a distance of 830 m from his office. He drives home without having to make a detour. How far, in kilometres, has he driven during the day?

8) Calculate the amount of ribbon left on a reel containing 50 m when the following lengths are cut: 50 cm, $\frac{1}{2}$ m, 2 m 30 cm and $4\frac{1}{4}$ m.

Multiplying and Dividing Metric Quantities

Multiplying and dividing metric quantities are done in the same way as the multiplication and division of decimal numbers.

Example 9 28 lengths of cloth each 3·8 m long are required for the manufacture of dresses. What total length of cloth is required?

Length required = 28 × 3·8 m

```
   28
   38
 ----
   84
  224
 ----
 1064
```

Placing the decimal point, we see that

total length of cloth required = 106·4 m.

THE METRIC SYSTEM

Example 10 How many lengths of string each 79 cm long can be cut from a ball containing 54 m and what length remains?

To do this problem we can either bring 79 cm to metres or we can convert 54 m into centimetres. Adopting the latter course we have,

$$54 \text{ m} = 54 \times 100 \text{ cm} = 5400 \text{ cm}$$

We now have to divide 5400 by 79, giving 68·35. Thus 68 whole lengths are obtained and 0·35 of a length remains. Hence:

$$\text{Length remaining} = 0.36 \times 79 \text{ cm} = 28.4 \text{ cm}$$

Therefore we can cut 68 lengths of string and a piece 28·4 cm long remains.

Exercise 40

1) 47 pieces of wood each 85 cm long are required. What total length of wood, in metres, is needed?

2) 158 lengths of cloth each 3·2 m long are required. Find the total length of cloth needed.

3) 27 lengths of cloth each 2 m 26 cm are to be cut from a roll containing 80 m. What length of cloth remains?

4) How many lengths of string each 58 cm long can be cut from a ball containing 30 m and how much string remains?

5) How many lengths of wood 18 cm long can be cut from a plank $6\frac{1}{2}$ m long?

6) Frozen peas are packed in boxes which contain 450 g. What mass of peas are needed to fill 2340 boxes?

7) Calculate the number of pieces of wallpaper each 2·7 m long that can be cut from a roll 17 m long.

8) 6 curtains are required each 2 m long. Allowing 5 cm for turnover at the top and 5 cm at the bottom of each curtain, how much material is needed?

Domestic Problems

The examples which follow illustrate the type of problems which most householders will experience from time to time.

Example 11 A room 12 m long and 7·2 m wide is to be carpeted with strips of carpet 90 cm wide running parallel to the length of the room. How many metres of carpet 90 cm wide are required?

It is a good idea to draw a diagram (Fig.5.1) so that we have a picture of the room in front of us.

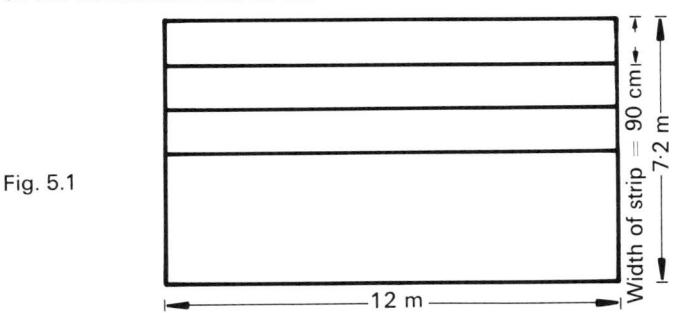

Fig. 5.1

$$\text{Since } 7{\cdot}2 \text{ m} = 7{\cdot}2 \times 100 \text{ cm} = 720 \text{ cm}$$
$$\text{number of strips required} = \frac{720}{90} = 8$$
$$\text{Total length of carpet 90 cm wide} = 8 \times 12 \text{ m} = 96 \text{ m}$$

Example 12   A room 6·2 m long, 8·3 m wide and 2·8 m high is to be papered. The width of the wallpaper is 80 cm and 7 pieces each 2·8 m long can be cut from each roll. Calculate the number of rolls of paper required. Neglect the allowance for doors and windows.

First make a drawing of the walls opened out as shown in Fig. 5.2. The total length of the walls is then seen to be $6{\cdot}2 + 8{\cdot}3 + 6{\cdot}2 + 8{\cdot}3 = 29$ m.

The problem now is to find how many times 80 cm will divide into 29 m. Converting 29 m into centimetres we have,

$$\text{number of pieces of wallpaper required} = \frac{2900}{80} = 36{\cdot}25$$

Hence we need 37 strips of paper and,

$$\text{number of rolls required} = \frac{37}{7} = 5{\cdot}3$$

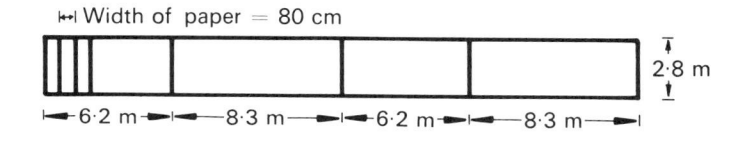

Fig. 5.2

Since we cannot buy 0·3 of a roll of wallpaper we must buy 6 rolls.

Example 13   Find the length of carpet required for a flight of 5 stairs having treads 21 cm wide and risers 19 cm high. Allow $1\frac{1}{4}$ m of carpet at the top and at the bottom.

First draw a diagram of the stairs (Fig. 5.3). Note that with the additional lengths at the top and bottom there are 5 risers but only 4 treads. Working in metres,

length of carpet required: 5 risers at 0·19 m = 0·95 m
                                  4 treads at 0·21 m = 0·84 m
                                  Top and bottom   = 2·50 m
                                                              4·29 m

                                                              say $4\frac{1}{2}$ m

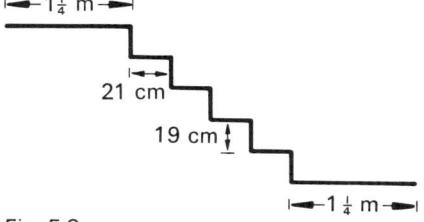

Fig. 5.3

THE METRIC SYSTEM

Exercise 41

1) A customer wishes to cover a room 8 m by 7·2 m with vinyl strips 120 cm wide. If the strips are to be 8 m long find the length of vinyl needed.

2) A housewife wishes to carpet a room measuring 10·8 m long by 12·4 m wide. She chooses carpet which is 90 cm wide. If the strips are laid to run parallel to the width of the room, what length of carpet is required?

3) A hall measuring 9 m by 1·8 m is to be carpeted with strips 60 cm wide. What length of carpet is required?

4) A staircase having 9 steps is to be carpeted. The treads are 21·5 cm wide and the risers are 20 cm high. Allowing 2 m at the top and $\frac{1}{2}$ m at the bottom, how much carpet is required?

5) A room is 8 m long, 6 m wide and 2·5 m high. The width of wallpaper is 80 cm and 7 strips each 2·5 m long can be cut from a roll. Calculate the number of rolls needed.

6) A certain wallpaper is available in rolls 17 m long and 75 cm wide. A room 6·3 m long and 5·8 m wide is to be papered with this wallpaper. If the room is 2·8 m high, how many rolls of paper are needed?

7) Calculate the length of stair carpet needed to cover a flight of 7 stairs if the treads are 32 cm wide and the risers 23 cm high. A length of $1\frac{1}{2}$ m is to be allowed at the top and at the bottom.

Mental Test 5

Try to answer the following questions without writing anything down except the answer.

1) Add 15·2 m and 25 cm.

2) Convert 579 mm into centimetres.

3) How many metres are there in 9·7 km?

4) How many centimetres are there in 3·76 m?

5) Add $5\frac{1}{2}$ m and 480 mm.

6) Multiply 9 cm by 20 and express the answer in metres.

7) 25 packets each having a mass of 360 mg are made up. What is their total mass in grams?

8) A length of 9 m and one of 6 m are cut from a roll of cloth 29 m long. How much cloth remains?

9) From a stock of 2000 kg of sugar the following amounts were sold: 200 kg, 150 kg and 90 kg. How much sugar remains?

10) 100 kg of flour were made up into 500 g bags. How many bags were there?

11) What is the total mass of sugar required to fill 800 cartons each containing 250 g. Answer in kilograms.

12) How many lengths of cord each 20 cm long can be cut from a length of 5 m?

Self Test 5

The answers to the following are either true or false. Write down the appropriate word.

1) 25 cm = 0·25 m

2) 4 cm = 0·4 m

3) 5 m = 500 mm

4) 2 km = 20 000 cm

5) 8000 mm = 80 m

6) 5 × 80 cm = 4 m

7) 20 × 200 g = 4 kg

8) 1·5 m ÷ 30 = 50 mm

9) 1000 m = 0·01 km
10) 13·5 kg = 13 500 g
11) 18 g = 18 000 mg
12) 12 × 50 g = 0·6 kg

13) 3·5 kg ÷ 50 = 7 g
14) 50 mm × 9 = 4·5 cm
15) 80 mg × 15 = 1·2 g
16) 50 mℓ × 30 = 1·5 ℓ

6. Areas

UNDERSTAND THE METRIC SYSTEM OF UNITS AS CURRENTLY IN USE IN BUSINESS

Perform calculations of the area of rectilinear figures.

Unit of Length

In Chapter 5 we saw that the standard unit of length is the metre (abbreviation: m) and that it is split up into smaller units as follows:

1 metre (m) = 10 decimetres (dm)
            = 100 centimetres (cm)
            = 1000 millimetres (mm)

Units of Area

The area of a plane figure is measured by seeing how many square units it contains. 1 square metre is the area contained inside a square which has a side of 1 metre (Fig. 6.1). Similarly 1 square centimetre is the area inside a square whose side is 1 cm and 1 square millimetre is the area inside a square whose side is 1 mm.

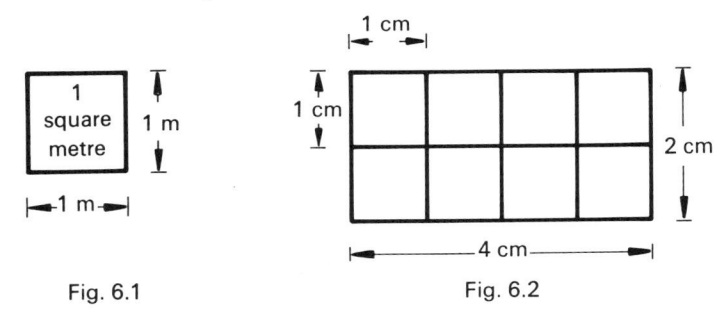

Fig. 6.1

Fig. 6.2

The standard abbreviations for units of area are:

square metre   = m^2
square centimetre = cm^2
square millimetre = mm^2

Area of a Rectangle

The rectangle (Fig. 6.2) has been divided into 4 rows of 2 squares, each square having an area of 1 cm^2. The rectangle, therefore, has an area of 4×2 cm^2 = 8 cm^2. All that we have done to find the area is to multiply the length by the breadth. The same rule will apply to any rectangle. Hence:

Area of rectangle = length × breadth

Example 1   A carpet measures 5·2 m by 6·3 m. What is its area?

Area = length × breadth = 5·2 × 6·3 = 32·76 m²

Example 2   Find the area of a piece of sheet metal measuring 184 cm by 73 cm. Express the answer in square metres.

In problems of this type it is best to express each of the dimensions in metres before attempting to find the area. Thus:

$$184 \text{ cm} = 1\cdot84 \text{ m and } 73 \text{ cm} = 0\cdot73 \text{ m}$$

The area of sheet metal = 1·84 × 0·73 = 1·3432 m²

Example 3   A room 9·3 m long and 7·6 m wide is to be carpeted so as to leave a surround 50 cm wide as shown in Fig. 6.3. Find the area of the surround.

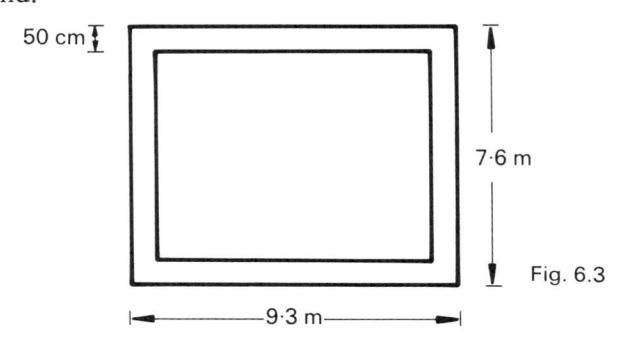

Fig. 6.3

The easiest way of solving this problem is to find the area of the room and subtract from it the area of the carpet.

Area of room   = 9·3 × 7·6 = 70·68 m²
Area of carpet = 8·3 × 6·6 = 54·78 m²
Area of surround = 70·68 − 54·78 = 15·90 m²

The areas of may shapes can be found by splitting the shape up into rectangles and finding the area of each rectangle separately. The area of the shape is then found by adding the areas of the separate rectangles together.

Example 4   Find the area of the shape shown in Fig. 6.4.

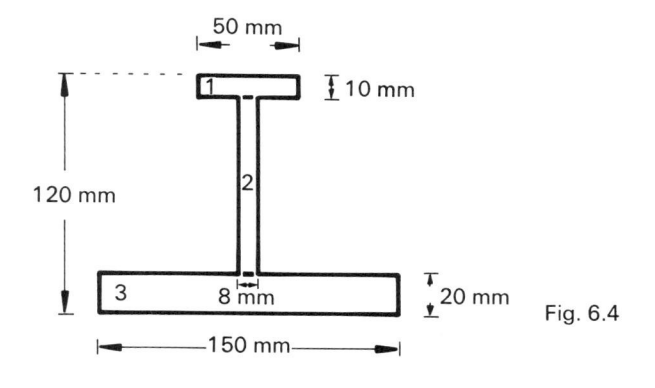

Fig. 6.4

AREAS

The shape can be divided up into three rectangles as shown in the diagram.

$$\text{Area of shape} = \text{area of 1} + \text{area of 2} + \text{area of 3}$$
$$= (50 \times 10) \text{ mm}^2 + (90 \times 8) \text{ mm}^2 + (150 \times 20) \text{ mm}^2$$
$$= 500 \text{ mm}^2 + 720 \text{ mm}^2 + 3000 \text{ mm}^2 = 4220 \text{ mm}^2$$

Exercise 42

1) Find the areas of the following rectangles:
   (a) 7 cm by 8 cm
   (b) 20 mm by 11 mm
   (c) 18 m by 35 m.

2) A piece of wood is 3·7 m long and 28 cm wide. What is its area in square metres?

3) A rectangular piece of metal is 198 cm long and 88 cm wide. What is its area in square metres?

4) A room 5·8 m long and 4·9 m wide is to be covered with vinyl. What area of vinyl is needed?

5) What is the total area of the walls of a room which is 6·7 m long, 5·7 m wide and 2·5 m high?

6) A rectangular lawn is 32 m long and 23 m wide. A path 1·5 m wide is made around the lawn. What is the area of the path?

7) A room 8·5 m long and 6·3 m wide is to be carpeted to leave a surround 60 cm wide around the carpet. What is:
   (a) the area of the room?
   (b) the area of the carpet?
   (c) the area of the surround?

8) Find the areas of the shapes shown in Fig. 6.5.

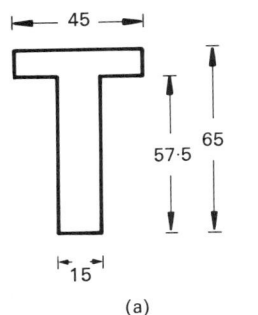

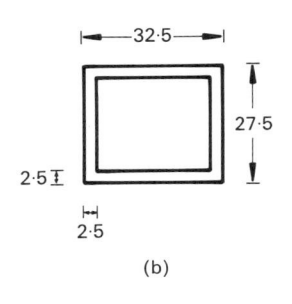

Fig. 6.5 (all dimensions in mm)

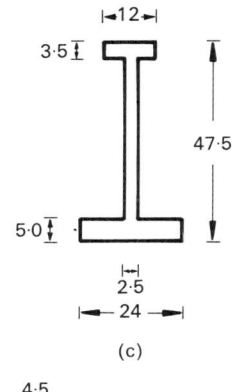

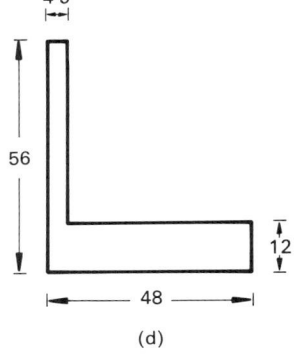

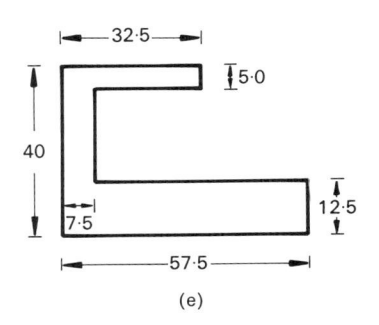

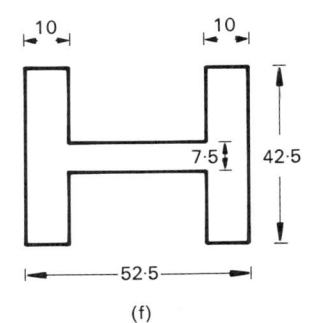

The Square

A square is a rectangle with all its sides equal in length. Hence:

$$\text{area of square} = \text{side} \times \text{side} = \text{side}^2$$

Example 5   A square has a side 5 cm long. What is its area?

$$\text{Area} = 5 \times 5 = 25 \text{ cm}^2$$

The Parallelogram

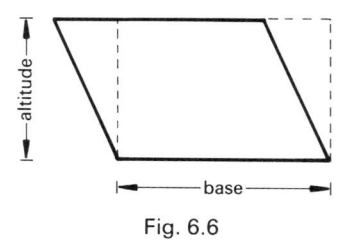

Fig. 6.6

A parallelogram is a plane figure bounded by four straight lines whose opposite sides are parallel (Fig. 6.6). A parallelogram is, in effect, a rectangle pushed out of square as shown in Fig. 6.6 where the equivalent rectangle is shown dotted. Hence:

$$\text{area of parallelogram} = \text{length of base} \times \text{vertical height}$$

Example 6   Find the area of a parallelogram whose base is 15 cm long and whose altitude is 8 cm.

$$\text{Area} = 15 \times 8 = 120 \text{ cm}^2$$

Exercise 43

1) A room is 5·4 m long and 4·2 m wide. It takes 1575 square tiles to cover the floor. Calculate the area of each tile.

2) How many square tiles each 15 cm square are needed to cover a floor 4·5 m long by 12 m wide?

3) A householder makes a square lawn in his garden which has a side of 12 m. If the plot of ground is 15 m by 14 m, what area is left?

4) Find the area of a parallelogram whose base is 7 cm long and whose vertical height is 8 cm.

5) What is the area of a parallelogram whose base is 7 cm long and whose altitude is 65 cm? Give the answer in square metres.

6) The area of a parallelogram is 64 m². Its base is 16 m long. Calculate its altitude.

7) A parallelogram has an area of 25·92 cm². Its altitude is 3·6 cm. Find its length of base.

8) Fig. 6.7 shows a steel section. Find its area in square centimetres.

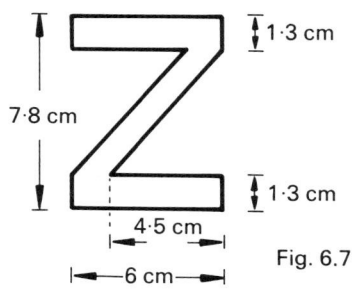

Fig. 6.7

Area of a Triangle

The diagonal of the parallelogram shown in Fig. 6.8 splits the parallelogram into two equal triangles. Hence:

$$\text{area of triangle} = \tfrac{1}{2} \times \text{base} \times \text{vertical height}$$

Sometimes the vertical height is called the altitude and:

$$\text{area of triangle} = \tfrac{1}{2} \times \text{base} \times \text{altitude}$$

Example 7 A triangle has a base 5 cm long and a vertical height of 12 cm. Calculate its area.

$$\text{Area of triangle} = \tfrac{1}{2} \times \text{base} \times \text{height} = \tfrac{1}{2} \times 5 \times 12 = 30 \text{ cm}^2$$

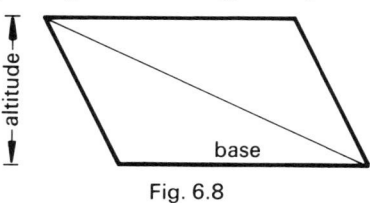

Fig. 6.8

Area of a Trapezium

A trapezium is a plane figure bounded by four straight lines which has one pair of parallel sides (Fig. 6.9).

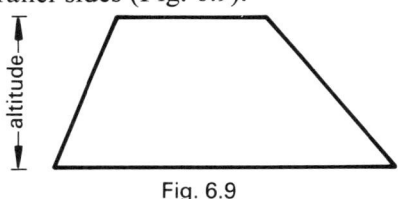

Fig. 6.9

Area of trapezium = $\tfrac{1}{2}$ the sum of the lengths of the parallel sides × the distance between them

Example 8 The parallel sides of a trapezium are 12 cm and 16 cm long. The distance between the parallel sides is 9 cm. What is the area of the trapezium?

$$\text{Area of trapezium} = \tfrac{1}{2} \times (12+16) \times 9 = \tfrac{1}{2} \times 28 \times 9 = 126 \text{ cm}^2$$

Exercise 44

1) Find the area of a triangle whose base is 18 cm and whose altitude is 12 cm.

2) Find the area of a triangle whose base is 7·5 cm and whose altitude is 5·9 cm.

3) Find the area of a trapezium whose parallel sides are 7 cm and 9 cm long and whose altitude is 5 cm.

4) The parallel sides of a trapezium are 15 cm and 9·8 cm long. If the distance between the parallel sides is 7·6 cm, what is the area of the trapezium?

5) The area of a trapezium is 500 cm² and its parallel sides are 35 cm and 65 cm long. Find the altitude of the trapezium.

6) Find the area of a trapezium whose parallel sides are 75 mm and 82 mm and whose vertical height is 39 mm. Give the answer in square centimetres.

Mensuration of the Circle

The names of the main parts of a circle are shown in Fig. 6.10. The value

$$\frac{\text{circumference}}{\text{diameter}} = 3\cdot141\ 59\ \ldots\ldots\ldots$$

The exact value has never been worked out but for most problems a value of 3·142 is sufficiently accurate when working in decimals. When working in fractions a value of $\frac{22}{7}$ can be taken.

The value $\frac{\text{circumference}}{\text{diameter}}$ is so important that it has been given the special symbol π (the Greek letter pi). We take π as being 3·142 or $\frac{22}{7}$.

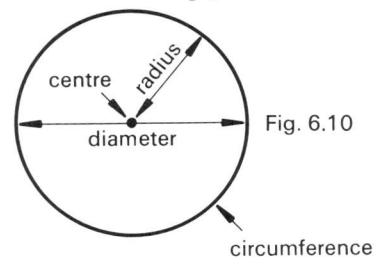

Fig. 6.10

Since $\frac{\text{circumference}}{\text{diameter}} = \pi$

circumference = $\pi \times$ diameter

or circumference = $2 \times \pi \times$ radius

Example 9 The diameter of a circle is 300 mm. What is its circumference?

Circumference = $\pi \times 300 = 3\cdot142 \times 300 = 942\cdot6$ mm

Example 10 The radius of a circle is 14 cm. What is its circumference?

Circumference = $2 \times \pi \times$ radius = $2 \times \frac{22}{7} \times 14 = 88$ cm

Example 11 A wheel 700 mm diameter makes 30 revolutions. How far does a point on the rim travel?

Distance travelled in 1 revolution
 = $\pi \times$ diameter = $\frac{22}{7} \times 700 = 2200$ mm

Distance travelled in 30 revolutions
 = $30 \times 2200 = 66\,000$ mm = 66 m

Exercise 45

Find the circumference of the following circles:

1) Radius 21 cm
2) Radius 350 mm
3) Radius 43 m
4) Radius 3·16 cm
5) Diameter 28 cm
6) Diameter 85 mm
7) Diameter 8·423 m
8) Diameter 1400 mm

AREAS

9) A wheel has a diameter of 560 mm. How far, in metres, will a point on the rim travel in 50 revolutions?

10) A circular flower bed has a circumference of 64 m. What is its radius?

11) 8 circular cushion covers whose radius is 60 cm are to be decorated with braiding around their circumference. How many metres of braiding is needed?

12) A pond which is circular has a circumference of 12·62 m. What is its radius?

13) Find the diameter of a circle whose circumference is 110 cm.

14) Find the diameter of a circle whose circumference is 956 mm.

Area of a Circle

It can be shown that:

$$\text{Area of circle} = \pi \times \text{radius}^2$$

Example 12 Find the area of a circle whose radius is 30 cm.

$$\text{Area of circle} = \pi \times 30^2 = 3\cdot142 \times 900 = 2827\cdot8 \text{ cm}^2$$

Example 13 Find the area of a circle whose diameter is 28 cm.

Since diameter = 28 cm, radius = 14 cm

$$\text{Area of circle} = \pi \times \text{radius}^2 = \tfrac{22}{7} \times 14^2 = 616 \text{ cm}^2$$

Example 14 Find the area of the annulus shown in Fig. 6.11.

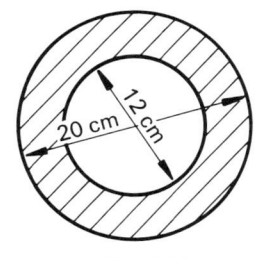

Fig. 6.11

Outer radius = 10 cm; inner radius = 6 cm
Area of outer circle = $\pi \times 10^2$ = 314·2 cm²
Area of inner circle = $\pi \times 6^2$ = 113·1 cm²
Area of annulus   = 314·2 − 113·1 = 201·1 cm²

Exercise 46

Find the areas of the following circles:

1) 14 cm radius
2) 350 mm radius
3) 2·82 m radius
4) 42 cm diameter
5) 7·78 m diameter
6) 197·6 mm diameter
7) An annulus has an inside radius of 6 cm and an outside radius of 9 cm. Calculate its area.
8) A copper pipe has a bore of 32 mm

and an outside diameter of 42 mm. Find the area of its cross section.

9) A pond having a diameter of 36 m has to have a path 1 m wide laid around its circumference. What is the area of the path?

10) A circular flower bed is to have a path laid around its circumference. If the flower bed has a diameter of 60 m and the path is to be $1\frac{1}{2}$ m wide, find the area of the path.

Summary

1) The area of a figure is measured by seeing how many square units it contains.
   1 square metre is the area contained in a square of 1 m side.
   1 square centimetre is the area inside a square whose side is 1 cm.
   1 square millimetre is the area inside a square whose side is 1 mm.
2) Area of rectangle = length × breadth.
3) Area of square = side².
4) Area of parallelogram = base × altitude.
5) Area of triangle = $\frac{1}{2}$ × base × altitude.
6) Area of trapezium = $\frac{1}{2}$ of the sum of the parallel sides × altitude.
7) Circumference of a circle = 2 × π × radius = π × diameter.
8) Area of circle = π × radius²

Mental Test 6

1) What is the area of a rectangle 8 cm long and 5 cm wide?

2) A square has an area of 36 m². What is the length of its side?

3) A rectangle has an area of 48 cm². It is 8 cm long. What is its width?

4) A parallelogram has a base 12 cm long and an altitude of 8 cm. What is its area?

5) A parallelogram has an area of 700 mm². Its altitude is 35 mm. Find its length of base.

6) A triangle has a base of 8 cm long and an altitude of 4 cm. What is its area?

7) A triangle has an area of 18 m² and a base 9 m long. What is its altitude?

8) A trapezium has an altitude of 6 cm and the parallel sides are 3 cm and 7 cm long. What is its area?

9) Find the circumference of a circle whose radius is 7 cm.

10) Find the circumference of a circle whose diameter is 28 cm.

11) Find the area of a circle whose radius is 7 cm.

Self-Test 6

1) A rectangle has a length of 80 mm and a width of 30 mm. Its area is therefore:
    a 240 mm²   **b** 2400 mm²
    c 24 cm²   **d** 240 cm²

2) A triangle has an altitude of 100 mm and a base of 50 mm. Its area is:
    a 2500 mm²   **b** 5000 mm²
    c 25 cm²   **d** 50 cm²

3) A parallelogram has a base 10 cm long and a vertical height of 5 cm. Its area is:
 a 25 cm²   b 50 cm²
 c 2500 mm²   d 5000 mm²

4) A trapezium has parallel sides whose lengths are 18 cm and 22 cm. The distance between the parallel sides is 10 cm. Hence the area of the trapezium is:
 a 400 cm²   b 200 cm²
 c 3960 cm²   d 495 cm²

5) The area of a circle is given by the formula:
 a $2 \times \pi \times \text{radius}^2$ b $2 \times \pi \times \text{radius}$
 c $\pi \times \text{radius}^2$ d $\pi \times \text{radius}$

6) The circumference of a circle is given by the formula:
 a $\pi \times \text{radius}^2$ b $2 \times \pi \times \text{radius}$
 c $\pi \times \text{radius}$ d $\pi \times \text{diameter}$

7) A ring has an outside diameter of 8 cm and an inside diameter of 4 cm. Its area is:
 a $\pi \times 8^2 - \pi \times 4^2$ b $8 \times \pi - 4 \times \pi$
 c $4 \times \pi - 2 \times \pi$ d $\pi \times 4^2 - \pi \times 2^2$

8) A wheel has a diameter of 70 cm. The number of revolutions that it will make in travelling 55 km is:
 a 2500   b 5000   c 50 000   d 25 000

9) A rectangular plot of ground is 40 m long and 80 m wide. Its area is:
 a 320 m²   b 3200 m²
 c 32 000 000 cm²   d 32 000 cm²

7. The Imperial System of Units

IMPERIAL SYSTEM OF UNITS
Convert units within the Imperial System.

Introduction

Although, in some instances, the Imperial system of units has been replaced by the Metric system, in many businesses it is still used. In this chapter the Imperial system for length, mass and capacity are discussed.

The Imperial System for Length

$$12 \text{ inches (in)} = 1 \text{ foot (ft)}$$
$$3 \text{ feet (ft)} = 1 \text{ yard (yd)}$$
$$1760 \text{ yards (yd)} = 1 \text{ mile}$$

Example 1   Convert 19 ft into inches.
$$1 \text{ ft} = 12 \text{ in}$$
$$19 \text{ ft} = 12 \times 19 = 228 \text{ in}$$

Example 2   Convert 2160 in into yards.
$$1 \text{ yd} = 3 \text{ ft} = 3 \times 12 = 36 \text{ in}$$
$$2160 \text{ in} = \frac{2160}{36} = 60 \text{ yd}$$

The Imperial System for Mass (or Weight)

$$16 \text{ ounces (oz)} = 1 \text{ pound (lb)}$$
$$112 \text{ pounds (lb)} = 1 \text{ hundredweight (cwt)}$$
$$20 \text{ hundredweight (cwt)} = 1 \text{ ton}$$

Example 3   Convert 4 ton 3 cwt into pounds.
$$4 \text{ ton } 3 \text{ cwt} = (4 \times 20) + 3 = 83 \text{ cwt}$$
$$1 \text{ cwt} = 112 \text{ lb}$$
$$83 \text{ cwt} = 83 \times 112 = 9296 \text{ lb}$$

Example 4   Convert 272 oz into pounds.
$$16 \text{ oz} = 1 \text{ lb}$$
$$272 \text{ oz} = \frac{272}{16} \text{ lb} = 17 \text{ lb}$$

The Imperial System for Capacity

$$20 \text{ fluid ounces (fl oz)} = 1 \text{ pint (pt)}$$
$$8 \text{ pints (pt)} = 1 \text{ gallon (gal)}$$

Example 5   Convert 480 fl oz. into gallons.

$$20 \text{ fl oz} = 1 \text{ pt}$$
$$480 \text{ fl oz} = \frac{480}{20} = 24 \text{ pt}$$
$$8 \text{ pt} = 1 \text{ gal}$$
$$24 \text{ pt} = \frac{24}{8} = 3 \text{ gal}$$

Conversion from Imperial Units into Metric Units

$$1 \text{ inch (in)} = 2.54 \text{ centimetres (cm)}$$
$$1 \text{ yard (yd)} = 0.9144 \text{ metre (m)}$$
$$1 \text{ pint (pt)} = 0.5682 \text{ litre } (\ell)$$
$$1 \text{ pound (lb)} = 0.4536 \text{ kilogram (kg)}$$

Example 6   Convert 8 yd 7 in into metres.

$$1 \text{ yd} = 0.9144 \text{ m}$$
$$8 \text{ yd} = 8 \times 0.9144 = 7.3152 \text{ m}$$
$$1 \text{ in} = 2.54 \text{ cm}$$
$$7 \text{ in} = 7 \times 2.54 = 17.78 \text{ cm} = 0.1778 \text{ m}$$
$$\therefore \quad 8 \text{ yd } 7 \text{ in} = 7.3152 + 0.1778 = 7.4930 \text{ m}$$

Example 7   Convert 7 pt 13 fl oz into litres.

$$1 \text{ pt} = 0.5682 \ \ell$$
$$7 \text{ pt} = 7 \times 0.5682 \ \ell = 3.9774 \ \ell$$
$$13 \text{ fl oz} = \frac{13}{20} \text{ pt} = \frac{13}{20} \times 0.5682$$
$$= 0.65 \times 0.5682 = 0.3693 \ \ell$$
$$\therefore \quad 7 \text{ pt } 13 \text{ fl oz} = 3.9774 + 0.3693 = 4.3467 \ \ell$$

Areas of Rectilinear Figures

As shown in Chapter 6,

area of rectangle = length × breadth
area of square = side²
area of triangle = ½ × base × altitude
area of parallelogram = base × altitude
area of trapezium = ½ the sum of the lengths of the parallel sides × distance between them
circumference of circle = π × diameter
= 2 × π × radius
area of circle = π × radius²

Units of Area

1 sq yard (yd²) is the area contained in a square with a side of 1 yard.
1 square foot (ft²) is the area contained in a square with a side of 1 foot.
1 square inch (in²) is the area contained in a square with a side of 1 inch.

Example 8 A carpet measures 5 yd × 4 yd. What is its area?

$$\text{Area} = \text{length} \times \text{breadth} = 5 \times 4 = 20 \text{ yd}^2$$

Example 9 A triangle has a base 6 in long and an altitude of 5 in. What is its area?

$$\text{Area} = \tfrac{1}{2} \times \text{base} \times \text{height} = \tfrac{1}{2} \times 6 \times 5 = 15 \text{ in}^2$$

Exercise 47

1) Convert into inches:
   (a) 14 ft   (b) 9 yd
   (c) 12 yd 2 ft

2) Convert into yards:
   (a) 9 ft 2 in   (b) 149 in
   (c) 2½ miles   (d) 1764 in

3) Convert into gallons:
   (a) 25 pt   (b) 16 pt 3 fl oz
   (c) 58 fl oz

4) Convert into inches:
   (a) 27 cm   (b) 3·06 m

5) Convert into litres:
   (a) 3 gal   (b) 6·2 pt
   (c) 5 fl oz

6) Convert into pounds:
   (a) 4·6 ton   (b) 8·3 cwt

7) Convert into kilograms:
   (a) 2·15 ton   (b) 27·3 lb
   (c) 14 oz   (d) 9·1 cwt

8) Convert into metres:
   (a) 5·4 in   (b) 3 ft 4 in
   (c) 19·4 yd

9) Find the area of the shape shown in Fig. 7.1.

10) Find the area of a parallelogram whose base is 9 in and whose altitude is 16 in.

11) A room 13·4 ft long and 11·8 ft wide is to be carpeted so as to leave a surround 25 in wide all round. Find the area of carpet needed in square yards.

12) Find the area of the trapezium shown in Fig. 7.2.

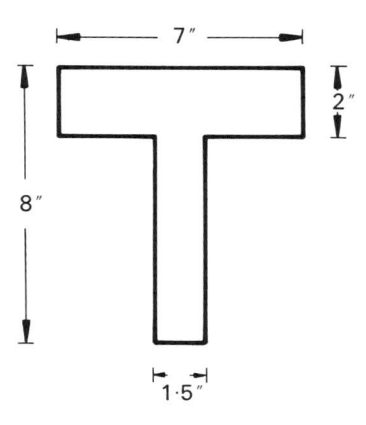

Fig. 7.1

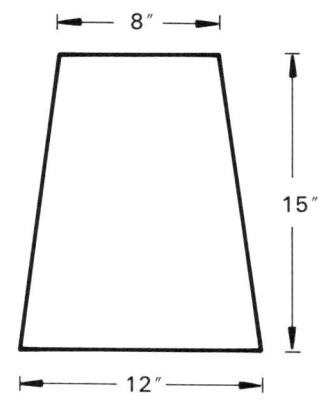

Fig. 7.2

THE IMPERIAL SYSTEM OF UNITS 65

13) A triangle has an altitude of 5 cm and a base 8 cm long. Calculate its area in square inches.

14) A circle has a diameter of 3·2 ft. What is its area?

15) Figure 7.3 shows a pipe. What is the area of metal in its cross-section?

16) A wheel has a radius of 2 ft. What is its circumference?

Mental Test 7

1) If 1 kilometre is $\frac{5}{8}$ of a mile, how many kilometres is 2 miles?

2) 5 inches is about $12\frac{1}{2}$ cm. How many centimetres is equal to 1 inch?

3) 1 pint is approximately 0·56 litre. How many litres are there in a gallon?

4) 1 lb = 450 g approximately. How many kilograms in 10 lb?

5) 1 ft = 0·3 m approximately. How many metres and centimetres in 25 ft?

6) 1 mm = 0·04 in approximately. How many inches in 200 mm?

7) 20 fluid ounces = 1 pint and 1 pint = 0·6 litres approx. How many litres do 60 fluid ounces equal?

8) 1 gallon = $4\frac{1}{2}$ litres approx. How many pints equal 1 litre?

9) 1 ton = 1000 kg approx. How many kilograms equal 8 tons?

10) 1 oz = 28 g approx. How many grams equal $\frac{1}{2}$ lb?

Self-Test 7

State the letter corresponding to the correct answer.

1) 5 pounds is equal to:
   a 800 oz   b 8 oz   c 80 oz
   d $\frac{5}{16}$ oz   e $\frac{16}{5}$ oz

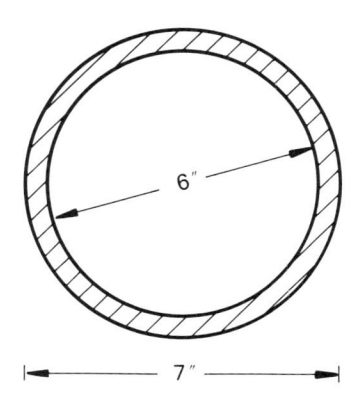

Fig. 7.3

2) 20 fluid ounces = 1 pint. Therefore 30 gallons, in fluid ounces, is:
   a $\frac{2}{3}$ b 600   c 160
   d 480   e 4800

3) 1 yard = 0·9 metre approx. Hence 1 inch is about:
   a $\frac{1}{4}$ b $\frac{1}{40}$ m   c 4 m
   d 40 m   e $\frac{3}{10}$ m

4) 8 inches = 200 mm approx. Therefore 2 inches is about:
   a 50 mm   b $\frac{1}{50}$ mm   c 100 mm
   d 25 mm   e $\frac{16}{200}$

5) 1 foot = 0·3 m approx. Hence 3 square feet are equal to:
   a 0·9 m²   b 0·09 m²   c $\frac{10}{3}$ m²
   d 10 m²   e 0·27 m²

6) 1 metre = 1·3 yards. How many yards in 30 m?
   a 39   b 3·9   c 390
   d $\frac{13}{300}$ e $\frac{300}{13}$

7) 1 litre = $1\frac{3}{4}$ pint. Hence 4 litres is equal to:
   a $\frac{16}{7}$ pints   b 7 pints   c $\frac{1}{7}$ pints
   d $\frac{16}{28}$ pints   e $\frac{7}{16}$ pints

8) 1 tonne = 1000 kg and 1 lb = 454 g. How many pounds equal 1 tonne?
   a 4540   b $\frac{1000 \times 1000}{454}$
   c $\frac{454}{1000}$ d $\frac{454}{1000 \times 1000}$
   e 45 400

8. Electronic Calculators

UNDERSTAND THE PURPOSE AND USE OF APPROXIMATIONS IN BUSINESS

Estimate the approximate value of arithmetic expressions.
Limit any answer to a numerical problem to a reasonable number of significant figures.
Question the validity of any solution to a numerical problem.
Reject an answer which is not feasible.
Make appropriate and effective use of calculators.

Introduction

A great deal of time and effort is often expended in arithmetic calculations even when logarithms are used. Much of this time and effort may be saved by using one of the electronic calculators. There are many types on the market but for most of us, a calculator which will add, subtract, multiply and divide is good enough.

The keyboard of a calculator has 10 number keys marked 0, 1, 2, 3, 4, 5, 6, 7, 8 and 9. There is also a decimal point. In the case of a simple calculator there are four function keys $+$, $-$, $\times$ and $\div$ and also an $=$ key. There is always a clear key, usually marked C, which is used to clear the display. Before each calculation it is safer to depress the C key.

Example 1 To find the value of $9{\cdot}632+18{\cdot}564-12{\cdot}768$.

Keyboard setting	Display
9 . 6 3 2	9·632
+ 1 8 . 5 6 4 =	28·196
− 1 2 . 7 6 8 =	15·428

Hence $9{\cdot}632+18{\cdot}564-12{\cdot}768 = 15{\cdot}428$

Note that when performing arithmetical operations the order of pressing the keys is always *FUNCTION EQUALS*.

ELECTRONIC CALCULATORS

Some calculators do not require the use of the = key when the sequence is followed by one of the functions +, −, × or ÷. The sequence of operations is then:

Keyboard setting	Display
9 . 6 3 2 +	9·632
1 8 . 5 6 4 −	28·196
1 2 . 7 6 8 =	15·428

Limiting the Answer to a Reasonable Number of Significant Figures

Most calculators have an 8 figure display but the answer can be given to any number of significant figures up to 8. However, an answer to a calculation should not contain more significant figures than the least number of significant figures used amongst the given numbers.

Example 2 Find the value of $7·231 \times 1·24 \times 1·3$ each number being correct to the number of significant figures shown.

Using a calculator,
$$7·231 \times 1·24 \times 1·3 = 11·656\,372$$

The least number of significant figures used amongst the given numbers is 2 (for the number 1·3). Hence the answer should only be stated correct to 2 significant figures.

$$\therefore \quad 7·231 \times 1·24 \times 1·3 = 12 \text{ correct to 2 significant figures}$$

Example 3 Find the value of $\dfrac{0·7285 \times 0.062\,53}{0·0281}$ each number being correct to the number of significant figures shown.

Using a calculator,
$$\frac{0·7285 \times 0·062\,53}{0·0281} = 1·621\,106\,9$$

However, the least number of significant figures amongst the numbers used in the calculation is 3 (for the number 0·0281). Hence the answer is 1·62, correct to 3 significant figures.

Rough Checks and the Feasibility of an Answer

It was shown (on page 29) that an answer to a calculation can be checked by using approximate numbers. When using a calculator a rough check should always be made to make sure that the answer is feasible.

Example 4 A calculator showed that $\dfrac{27 \cdot 5 \times 31 \cdot 32}{11 \cdot 2 \times 2 \cdot 94} = 26 \cdot 16$. Is this answer feasible?

For purposes of a rough check we will take $27 \cdot 5 \simeq 27$, $31 \cdot 32 \simeq 30$, $11 \cdot 2 \simeq 10$ and $2 \cdot 94 \simeq 3$. (Note that the symbol $\simeq$ means 'is approximately equal to'.)

Rough check $= \dfrac{27 \times 30}{10 \times 3} = 27$.

Hence the answer is feasible because the rough check shows that the answer given is of the right size.

Example 5 A calculator showed that $\dfrac{0 \cdot 563 \times 0 \cdot 621}{0 \cdot 0362} = 0 \cdot 966$. Is this answer feasible?

Performing a rough check: $\dfrac{0 \cdot 5 \times 0 \cdot 6}{0 \cdot 03} = 10$.

Hence the given answer is not feasible and must be rejected. On performing the calculation again, the answer is found to be 9·66 which agrees with the rough check.

Rearranging a Problem to Ease Calculation

It is sometimes necessary to change the order in which the arithmetic operations of a problem are performed so that the problem may be performed completely on the calculator.

Example 6 Using a calculator, evaluate $\dfrac{84 \cdot 3}{91 \cdot 2} + \dfrac{76 \cdot 51}{3 \cdot 84}$.

If we proceed as shown the operations are:

Keyboard setting   **Display**

| 8 | 4 | · | 3 | ÷ | 9 | 1 | · | 2 | = | 0·924 342 1

Write down display.

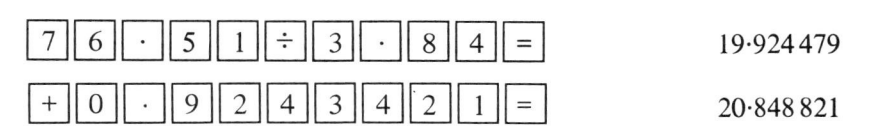

| 7 | 6 | · | 5 | 1 | ÷ | 3 | · | 8 | 4 | = | 19·924 479
| + | 0 | · | 9 | 2 | 4 | 3 | 4 | 2 | 1 | = | 20·848 821

Writing down a display in the middle of a calculation provides a fruitful source of error. It is better, if possible, to perform the calculation without writing down an intermediate result.

Our problem may be rewritten,

$$\frac{84\cdot3}{91\cdot2}+\frac{76\cdot51}{3\cdot84} = \left(\frac{84\cdot3\times3\cdot84}{91\cdot2}+76\cdot51\right)\div3\cdot84$$

The operations are:

Keyboard setting	Display
8 4 . 3 × 3 . 8 4 =	323·712
÷ 9 1 . 2 =	3·549 473 6
+ 7 6 . 5 1 =	80·059 473 6
÷ 3 . 8 4	20·848 821

The answer is 20·8 correct to 3 significant figures.

Overflow

If, as a result of a multiplication or addition the product or the sum contains more than 8 figures to the left of the decimal point then the machine will show the overflow indicator. To avoid this happening it pays to alternatively multiply and divide where this is possible or to express the numbers in standard form.

Example 7 Find the value of $\dfrac{289\cdot53\times6548\cdot79\times900\cdot876}{87\cdot63\times587\cdot26}$

If we perform the operations:

2 8 9 . 5 3 × 6 5 4 8 . 7 9

× 9 0 0 . 8 7 6 =

the overflow is brought into action.

However if we perform the operations like this:

2 8 9 . 5 3 ÷ 8 7 . 6 3

× 6 5 4 8 . 7 9 ÷ 5 8 7 . 2 6

× 9 0 0 . 8 7 6 =

we get the answer as 33 192·229 = 33 190 correct to 4 significant figures.

Rough check $= \dfrac{300\times7000\times900}{90\times600}$

$= 35000$

Hence the answer shown in the display of the calculator is feasible.

Calculating Powers of Numbers

Powers of numbers are very easy to obtain using some calculators.

Example 8   Find $6 \cdot 358^9$

| 6 | · | 3 | 5 | 8 | × | = | = | = | = | = | = | = | = |

(The display is 16 977 927)

gives the required operations. Note that the number of equal signs is always one less than the power of the number. (This method does not apply to all calculators. If it does not work for yours then perform the operations $6 \cdot 358 \times 6 \cdot 358 = \times 6 \cdot 358 =$ until nine multiplications have been performed.)

Since there are 4 significant figures in the number 6·358, the answer should only be stated to this degree of accuracy.

Hence $6 \cdot 358^9 = 16\,980\,000$

Rough check $\simeq 6^9 = 10\,000\,000$ (approx.)

Hence the answer of 16 980 000 is feasible.

Exercise 48

In each of the following questions, each number is correct to the number of significant figures shown. Evaluate each of them and perform a rough check to test the feasibility of your answer.

1) $17 \cdot 63 \times 20 \cdot 543$

2) $11 \cdot 26 \times 3 \cdot 178$

3) $15 \cdot 92 - 7 \cdot 63 + 2 \cdot 184$

4) $25 \cdot 14 \div 0 \cdot 36$

5) $\dfrac{95 \cdot 83 \times 6 \cdot 14}{8 \cdot 1795}$

6) $\dfrac{16 \cdot 13 \times 270 \cdot 52 \times 1 \cdot 2975}{15 \cdot 432 \times 139 \cdot 68}$

7) $\dfrac{11 \cdot 16}{7 \cdot 34} + \dfrac{2 \cdot 63}{8 \cdot 71}$

8) $\dfrac{0 \cdot 3786 \times 0 \cdot 0397}{31 \cdot 67 \times 1 \cdot 265}$

9) $\dfrac{0 \cdot 0146 \times 0 \cdot 7983 \times 643 \cdot 2}{33\,600 \times 11 \cdot 82}$

10) $11 \cdot 63 + \dfrac{17 \cdot 63}{0 \cdot 273}$

11) $\dfrac{12\,000 \times 280\,000}{19\,500 \times 26\,300}$

12) $\dfrac{0 \cdot 004\,79 \times 0 \cdot 000\,562}{0 \cdot 0563 \times 0 \cdot 0024}$

13) $(2 \cdot 673)^5$

14) $(11 \cdot 612)^7$

9. Percentages

UNDERSTAND THE NATURE AND FUNCTION OF PERCENTAGES
Convert fractions to percentages.
Convert decimals to fractions.
Calculate a stated percentage of a quantity.
Calculate the whole from a given percentage.
Express one quantity as a percentage of another.
Calculate percentage change.
Apply percentages in the solution to a variety of business problems.

When comparing fractions it is often convenient to express them with a denominator of a hundred. Thus:

$$\frac{1}{2} = \frac{50}{100}$$

$$\frac{2}{5} = \frac{40}{100}$$

Converting Fractions to Percentages

Fractions expressed with a denominator of 100 are called *percentages*. Thus:

$$\frac{1}{4} = \frac{25}{100} = 25 \text{ per cent}$$

$$\frac{3}{10} = \frac{30}{100} = 30 \text{ per cent}$$

The sign % is usually used instead of the words per cent.

To convert a fraction into a percentage we multiply it by 100.

Example 1

$$\frac{3}{4} = \frac{3}{4} \times 100\% = 75\%$$

$$\frac{17}{20} = \frac{17}{20} \times 100\% = 85\%$$

Exercise 49

Convert the following fractions to percentages:

1) $\frac{7}{10}$
2) $\frac{11}{20}$
3) $\frac{9}{25}$
4) $\frac{4}{5}$
5) $\frac{31}{50}$
6) $\frac{1}{4}$
7) $\frac{9}{10}$
8) $\frac{19}{20}$

Converting Decimals to Percentages

Decimal numbers may be converted into percentages by using the same rule. Thus:

$$0.3 = \frac{3}{10} = \frac{3}{10} \times 100 = 30\%$$

The same result is produced if we omit the intermediate step of turning 0·3 into a vulgar fraction and just multiply 0·3 by 100. Thus:

$$0.3 = 0.3 \times 100\% = 30\%$$

Example 2
$$0.56 = 0.56 \times 100\% = 56\%$$
$$0.683 = 0.683 \times 100\% = 68.3\%$$

Exercise 50

Convert the following decimal numbers into percentages:

1) 0·7
2) 0·73
3) 0·68
4) 0·813
5) 0·927
6) 0·333
7) 0·819

To convert a percentage into a fraction we divide by 100.

Example 3
$$45\% = \frac{45}{100} = 0.45$$
$$3.9\% = \frac{3.9}{100} = 0.039$$

Note that all we have done is to move the decimal point 2 places to the left.

Exercise 51

Convert the following percentages into decimal fractions:

1) 32%
2) 78%
3) 6%
4) 24%
5) 31·5%
6) 48·2%
7) 2·5%
8) 1·25%
9) 3·95%
10) 20·1%

Percentage of a Quantity

It is easy to find the percentage of a quantity if we first express the percentage as a fraction.

Example 4 1) What is 10% of 40?

Expressing 10% as a fraction it is $\frac{10}{100}$ and the problem then becomes: what is $\frac{10}{100}$ of 40?

$$10\% \text{ of } 40 = \frac{10}{100} \times 40 = 4$$

2) What is 25% of £50?

$$25\% \text{ of } £50 = \frac{25}{100} \times £50 = £12.50$$

3) 22% of a certain length is 55 cm. What is the complete length?

We have that 22% of the length = 55 cm

$$1\% \text{ of the length} = \frac{55}{22} \text{ cm} = 2.5 \text{ cm}$$

Now the complete length will be 100%, hence:

Complete length = 100×2.5 cm = 250 cm

Alternatively

22% of the length = 55 cm

$$\text{Complete length} = \frac{100}{22} \times 55 = \frac{100 \times 55}{22} = 250 \text{ cm}$$

4) What percentage is 37 of 264? Give the answer correct to 5 significant figures.

$$\text{Percentage} = \frac{37}{264} \times 100 = \frac{37 \times 100}{264} = 14.015\%$$

Exercise 52

1) What is:
 (a) 20% of 50
 (b) 30% of 80
 (c) 5% of 120
 (d) 12% of 20
 (e) 20·3% of 105
 (f) 3·7% of 68?

2) What percentage is:
 (a) 25 of 200
 (b) 30 of 150
 (c) 24 of 150
 (d) 29 of 178
 (e) 15 of 33?

Where necessary give the answer correct to 3 significant figures.

3) A girl scores 36 marks out of 60 in an examination. What is her percentage mark? If the percentage needed to pass the examination is 45% how many marks are needed to pass?

4) If 20% of a length is 23 cm what is the complete length?

5) Given that 13·3 cm is 15% of a certain length, what is the complete length?

6) What is:
 (a) 9% of £80
 (b) 12% of £110
 (c) 75% of £250?

7) Express the following statements in the form of a percentage:
 (a) 3 eggs are bad in a box containing 144 eggs.
 (b) In a school of 650 pupils, 20 are absent.
 (c) In a school of 980 pupils, 860 eat school lunches.

8) In a certain county the average number of children eating lunches at school was 29 336 which represents 74% of the total number of children attending school. Calculate the total number of children attending school in that county.

9) 23% of a consignment of bananas is bad. There are 34·5 kg of bad bananas. How many kilograms were there in the consignment?

10) A retailer accepts a consignment of 5000 ball point pens. He finds that 12% are faulty. How many faulty pens were there?

Percentage Profit and Loss

When a dealer buys or sells goods, the cost price is the price at which he buys the goods and the selling price is the price at which he sells the goods. If the selling price is greater than the cost price then a profit is made. The amount of profit is the difference between the selling price and the cost price. That is:

$$\text{Profit} = \text{selling price} - \text{cost price}$$

The profit per cent is always calculated on the cost price. That is:

$$\text{Profit \%} = \frac{\text{selling price} - \text{cost price}}{\text{cost price}} \times 100$$

If a loss is made the cost price is greater than the selling price. The loss is the difference between the cost price and the selling price. That is:

$$\text{Loss} = \text{cost price} - \text{selling price}$$

$$\text{Loss \%} = \frac{\text{cost price} - \text{selling price}}{\text{cost price}} \times 100$$

Example 5

1) A shopkeeper buys an article for £5·00 and sells it for £6·00. What is his profit per cent?

We are given: cost price = £5 and selling price = £6

$$\text{Profit \%} = \frac{6-5}{5} \times 100 = \frac{1}{5} \times 100 = 20\%$$

2) A dealer buys 20 articles at a total cost of £5. He sells them for 30 p each. What is his profit per cent?

Since £5 = 500 p, cost price per article = $\frac{500}{20}$ = 25 p

$$\text{Profit \%} = \frac{30-25}{25} \times 100 = \frac{5}{25} \times 100 = 20\%$$

3) A man buys a car for £1600 and sells it for £1200. Calculate his percentage loss.

Loss = cost price − selling price = £1600 − £1200 = £400

$$\text{Loss \%} = \frac{400}{1600} \times 100 = 25\%$$

Exercise 53

1) A shopkeeper buys an article for 80 p and sells it for £1. Calculate the percentage profit.

2) Calculate the profit per cent when:
   (a) Cost price is £1·50 and selling price is £1·80.
   (b) Cost price is 30 p and selling price is 35 p.

3) Calculate the loss per cent when:
   (a) Cost price is 75 p and selling price is 65 p.
   (b) Cost price is £6·53 and selling price is £5·88.

4) A greengrocer buys a box of 200 oranges for £5. He sells them for 3 p each. Calculate his percentage profit.

PERCENTAGES

5) A dealer buys 100 similar articles for £60 and sells them for 80 p each. Find his profit per cent.

6) A retailer buys 30 articles at 8 p each. Three are damaged and unsaleable but he sells the others at 10 p each. What is the profit per cent?

7) A car is bought for £1700 and sold for £1400. What is the loss per cent?

8) The price of coal has increased from £20 to £22 per 1000 kilograms. What is the percentage increase in the price of coal?

Mark Up

The mark up is the same as the percentage profit calculated on the cost price. That is:

$$\text{Mark up} = \frac{\text{selling price} - \text{cost price}}{\text{cost price}} \times 100$$

Examples 6

1) A butcher buys a 15 kilogram lamb for £15·00. He sells it at £1·30 per kilogram. Calculate the mark up.

$$\text{Cost price} = \frac{15}{15} = £1\cdot00 \text{ per kilogram}$$

Selling price = £1·30 per kilogram

$$\text{Mark up} = \frac{1\cdot30 - 1\cdot00}{1\cdot00} \times 100 = 30\%$$

2) Calculate the selling price of potatoes if they are bought for £5 per 50 kg bag and the mark up is 25%.

In questions of this type it is a good idea to set out the information in the form of a table, as shown below:

	Cost price	Profit	Selling price
%	100	25	125
p	10	$2\frac{1}{2}$	$12\frac{1}{2}$

Note that in problems on mark up the cost price is always 100% and that the selling price is the cost price plus the profit, in this case 100% + 25% = 125%. In the second row the cost price is $\frac{500}{50} = 10$ p per kilogram. The profit is $10 \times \frac{25}{100} = 2\frac{1}{2}$ p per kg whilst the selling price is $10 \text{ p} + 2\frac{1}{2} \text{ p} = 12\frac{1}{2}$ p per kg.

3) A retailer sells a dining table for £156. If his mark up is 30% find how much he paid for the table.

Drawing up a table as before, we have:

	Cost price	Profit	Selling price
%	100	30	130
£			156

So we have that $130\% = £156$. We now have to find 100%. We can use the unitary method. Thus:

$$130\% = £156$$
$$1\% = £\frac{156}{130}$$
$$100\% = £\frac{156}{130} \times 100 = £120$$

Hence the cost price is £120.

Exercise 54

1) A carpet shop buys carpet at £3 per metre length and sells it for £3·60 per metre. What is the mark up?

2) A greengrocer buys grapefruit at £16 for a box of 200. He sells them for 10 p each. Calculate his mark up.

3) A store buys dress material at £3·60 per metre length. If the mark up is to be 25% calculate the selling price of the material.

4) A department store buys washing machines for £180 each. Calculate the selling price of the machines if the mark up is 30%.

5) A dealer buys 20 secondhand electric fires for £50. His mark up is 50%. How much is his selling price for each fire?

6) A furniture shops sells dining chairs at £20 each. If the mark up is 25% what is the cost price of the chairs?

7) A carpet is sold to a customer for £98. If the mark up is 40%, find the cost price of the carpet.

8) A greengrocer sells oranges at 8 p each. If his mark up is $33\frac{1}{3}\%$ find how much was paid for a box of 100 oranges.

9) A baker has weekly takings of £1350. If his mark up is 20%, calculate his weekly profit.

10) A book shop has monthly sales of £6000. If the mark up is 30% calculate the monthly profit.

Margin

Although it is usual to calculate the profit as a percentage of the cost price it is much simpler for a retailer to calculate his profit as a percentage of the selling price. This is because his till shows the amount of his takings per day or per week and if his profit is calculated on the selling price it is easy to calculate his percentage profit. When the profit is stated as a percentage of the selling price it is called the *margin*.

Example 7 A retailer finds that a week's takings amount to £1200. His margin is 20%. Calculate his weekly profit, the mark up and the cost price of the goods sold.

Setting the information out in the form of a table we have:

PERCENTAGES

	Cost price	Profit	Selling price
%	80	20	100
£			1200

Note that in problems dealing with margin we make the selling price equal to 100%.

$$100\% = £1200$$
$$1\% = \frac{£1200}{100} = £12$$
$$20\% = £12 \times 20 = £240$$
$$80\% = £12 \times 80 = £960$$

Hence the profit is £240 and the cost price if £960. Hence:

$$\text{Mark up} = \frac{240}{960} \times 100 = 25\%$$

Relation Between Margin and Mark Up

The method of dealing with margins and mark up is best illustrated by means of an example.

Example 8 A grocer marks up his goods by 30%. What is his margin?

The easiest way is to assume that he sells goods which cost him £100. Then:

Profit = 30% of £100 = £30
Selling price = £100 + £30 = £130
Margin = $\frac{\text{profit}}{\text{selling price}} \times 100 = \frac{30}{130} \times 100 = 23 \cdot 08\%$

Exercise 55

1) A dealer finds that his weekly takings are £1500. If his margin is 20% calculate his weekly profit.

2) A retailer has daily takings of £250. If his margin is 25% calculate his profit, mark up, and the cost price of the goods sold.

3) A grocer works on a mark up of 40%. What is his margin?

4) A furniture store works on a margin of 20%. What is the mark up?

5) A firm has a profit margin of 40% on the goods it sells. If the firm makes a profit during one month of £9600 calculate the value of the goods sold.

6) A carpet shop works on a margin of 35%. What is the mark-up? If its sales during one week are £530, what profit has it made?

7) A grocer marks up the cost of butter which he sells by 30%. Calculate his margin as a percentage of the selling price.

8) A butcher buys a 15 kg lamb for £36 and he sells it for £3 per kg. Calculate his margin as a percentage of the selling price.

Gross and Net Profits

We have seen that the profit is found by subtracting the cost price from the selling price. This gives us the *gross profit*. However tradespeople usually have to take other expenses into account in calculating their *net profit*. For instance there will be wages to pay to assistants, running expenses for vans and other transport, rates, etc. These extra expenses are called *overheads*. In order to calculate the net profit these overheads must be subtracted from the gross profit. The total sales or takings are usually called the *turnover*.

$$\text{Gross profit} = \text{turnover} - \text{cost price}$$
$$\text{Net profit} = \text{gross profit} - \text{overheads}$$

Example 9 The sales of a store during a certain year were £35 000. The cost price of the goods sold was £22 000 and the overheads were £7000. Calculate:
(a) the gross profit and the net profit,
(b) the gross profit and net profit as a percentage of the turnover,
(c) the gross profit and the net profit as a percentage of the cost price.

(a) Gross profit = £35 000 − £22 000 = £13 000
    Net profit = £13 000 − £7000 = £6000

(b) Gross profit % = $\frac{13\,000}{35\,000} \times 100 = 37 \cdot 1\%$

    Net profit % = $\frac{6000}{35\,000} \times 100 = 17 \cdot 1\%$

(c) Gross profit % = $\frac{13\,000}{22\,000} \times 100 = 59 \cdot 1\%$

    Net profit % = $\frac{6000}{22\,000} \times 100 = 27 \cdot 3\%$

Exercise 56

1) The sales of a small business totalled £38 000 during a certain year. If the cost price of the goods sold was £23 000 and the overheads were £7000, find:

(a) the net profit and the gross profit,
(b) the net and gross profit expressed as a percentage of the turnover,
(c) the net profit and gross profit expressed as a percentage of the cost price.

2) A grocer sells goods to the value of £500 per week and in doing so makes a gross profit of 25%. If his overheads amount to £40 per week find:

(a) the net profit per week,
(b) the net profit per week expressed as a percentage of weekly sales.

3) A small shopkeeper expects to make a net profit of £4200 in a year's trading. During the year the cost price of the goods he sells amount to £18 000 and his overheads amount to £4000. Calculate his annual sales so that he can make the expected profit and express this net profit as a percentage of his annual sales.

4) The weekly sales of a confectioner amount to £700 per week and the cost price of his goods average out to £440 per week. He rents his shop at £56 per week and he pays an assistant £64 per week. Calculate:

(a) the net profit per week,
(b) the net profit expressed as a percentage of sales,

(c) the net profit expressed as a percentage of the cost price of the goods sold.

5) A chemist has total sales of £45 000 per year and the cost price of the goods he sells amount to £30 000 per year. His overheads consist of rates £450 per year, salaries £3000 per year, heating £530 per year and lighting £250 per year. Calculate:
(a) the gross profit,
(b) the overheads,
(c) the net profit,
(d) the net profit expressed as a percentage of the turnover,
(e) the net profit expressed as a percentage of the cost price.

Discount

When a customer buys an article from a retailer for cash he will often ask the retailer for a discount. This discount, which is usually a percentage of the selling price, is the amount which the retailer will take off his selling price thus reducing his profit.

Example 10 A music centre is offered for sale at £120. A customer is offered a 10% discount for cash. How much does the customer actually pay?

$$\text{Discount} = 10\% \text{ of } £120 = \frac{10}{100} \times £120 = £12$$

Amount paid by customer = £120 − £12 = £108

(*Alternatively:* since only 90% of the selling price is paid,

$$\text{Amount customer pays} = 90\% \text{ of } £120 = \frac{90}{100} \times £120 = £108)$$

Sometimes discounts are quoted as so much in the pound, for instance 5 p in the £1. If we remember that 5 p in the £1 is the same as 5% then the calculation of discounts is the same as that shown in Example 10.

Example 11 How much will a girl pay for goods priced at £12·50 if a discount of 8 p in the £1 is offered for cash?

8 p in £1 is the same as 8%

$$\text{Discount} = \frac{8}{100} \times £12 \cdot 50 = £1 \cdot 00$$

Amount paid by the girl = £12·50 − £1·00 = £11·50

Exercise 57

1) A chair marked for sale at £14 is sold for cash at a discount of 10%. What price did the customer pay?

2) A tailor charges £60 for a suit of clothes but allows a discount of 5% for cash. What is the cash price?

3) A grocer offers a discount of $2\frac{1}{2}\%$ to his customers provided their bills are paid within one week. If a bill of £14·50 is paid within one week, how much discount will the grocer allow?

4) A shop offers a discount of 5 p in the £1. How much discount will be allowed on a washing machine costing £225?

5) A furniture store offers a discount of 7 p in the £1 for cash sales. A customer buys a three piece suite priced at £785. How much will she actually pay?

Trade Discount

Trade discounts are discounts offered by a manufacturer, or a wholesaler to a retailer. The list price quoted by the manufacturer is the price at which the retailer is expected to sell the article. Trade discounts are usually of the order of 20%, 25% or $33\frac{1}{3}\%$.

Example 12 A manufacturer offers a trade discount of 25% to retailers. Calculate the price a retailer will pay for an article if it is listed by the manufacturer at £160.

$$\text{Trade discount} = 25\% \text{ of } £160 = \frac{25}{100} \times £160 = £40$$

$$\text{Price to retailer} = £160 - £40 = £120$$

Sometimes a manufacturer will offer an additional discount for an early settlement by the retailer.

Example 13 A manufacturer invoices his goods to a retailer less a trade discount of $33\frac{1}{3}\%$ and a further discount of 5% if the account is settled within 28 days. How much will the retailer actually pay for goods invoiced at £270 if he gets the benefit of both discounts?

First note that $33\frac{1}{3}\%$ is the same as $\frac{1}{3}$.

$$\text{Trade discount} = 33\frac{1}{3}\% \text{ of } £270 = \frac{1}{3} \text{ of } £270 = £90$$

$$\text{Price to retailer} = £270 - £90 = £180$$

$$\text{Cash discount} = 5\% \text{ of } £180 = \frac{5}{100} \times £180 = £9$$

$$\text{Amount retailer actually pays} = £180 - £9 = £171$$

(Note carefully that it is wrong to add the two discount percentages together thus saying that the total discount is $38\frac{1}{3}\%$. The actual total discount is $36\frac{2}{3}\%$.)

Sometimes problems occur in which we are told the discounts and the price the retailer pays. We are then asked to find the list or wholesale price.

Example 14 A housewife's grocery bill, after a deduction of a discount of 5%, amounts to £14·25. What is the gross amount of the bill?

Since the discount is 5% the amount paid is 95% of the gross amount. That is:

$$95\% = £14\!\cdot\!25$$

The gross amount is represented by 100%. Hence:

$$\text{Gross amount of bill} = \frac{100}{95} \times £14\!\cdot\!25 = £15$$

Example 15 A wholesaler allows a retailer a trade discount of 25% and a cash discount of 5% for immediate settlement. What is the wholesale price of goods for which the retailer pays £14·25?

Let wholesale price = £100
Less trade discount of 25% = 75% of £100 = £75
Less cash discount of 5% = 95% of £75 = £71·25

Hence the ratio:

wholesalers price : retailers price = 100 : 71·25

$$\text{wholesalers price} = \frac{100}{71 \cdot 25} \times £14 \cdot 25 = £20$$

Invoices with Discount

We have already dealt with invoices without discount on page 43. An invoice is a document which states the quantity, description and price of goods sold. It also gives details of any discounts and it is sent to the purchaser when the goods are despatched.

The following is a typical invoice:

INVOICE

No. 93

N. Green, Esq,
17 South St,
Cheltenham

25 Great St
London W1

Bought of S. Brown

Terms $2\frac{1}{2}$% one month

30 pairs shoes at £23·00 per pair	£690·00
20 pairs slippers at £8·80 per pair	£176·00
40 pairs plimsolls at £7·20 per pair	£288·00
	1154·00
Less 20% discount	230·80
	£923·20

N. Green now owes S. Brown 923·20 but if he pays the account within one month he will be allowed a further $2\frac{1}{2}$% discount. Hence the amount he will actually pay is $97\frac{1}{2}$% of £923·20 or £900·12.

Exercise 58

1) A manufacturer offers a discount of 25% of an article which is listed at £224. How much will a retailer pay for it?

2) A wholesaler's list price for an article is £15. If he offers a trade discount of $33\frac{1}{3}$%, how much will a retailer pay for the article?

3) A manufacturer offers a trade dis-

count of 25%. A retailer pays £150 for a certain item. What is the manufacturer's price?

4) A car is listed by a manufacturer at £8500. A garage owner buys it from the manufacturer for £5950. What is the trade discount per cent?

5) A retailer pays £203 to a wholesaler for goods on which the wholesaler allows a discount of $33\frac{1}{3}$%. What is the wholesaler's price?

6) A manufacturer allows a retailer a trade discount of 20% and a cash discount of 5% if payment is made within seven days. If the manufacturer's list price is £240, how much does the retailer pay if he gains the benefit of both discounts.

7) A wholesaler gives a trade discount of 25% to retailers and a cash discount of $2\frac{1}{2}$% provided settlement is made within one month. If a retailer pays £146·25, how much is the wholesaler's list price?

8) A car is listed at £3200 by the manufacturer. A retailer in buying the car is offered a trade discount of 25% together with a cash discount of 3% for settlement within 28 days. If the retailer is entitled to both discounts, how much does he pay the manufacturer?

9) A wholesaler allows a retailer a 20% trade discount and a·5% discount for prompt payment. What is the wholesale price for goods for which the retailer paid £7·60?

10) Prepare an invoice for the following:
50 pairs of double sheets at £18 per pair
30 pairs of single sheets at £16 per pair
80 pillowcases at £1·75 each
20 bedspreads at £17·55 each

The terms are 25% trade discount. If a cash discount of $2\frac{1}{2}$% is allowed for prompt payment, how much does a retailer pay for the goods?

11) Make out an invoice for the following. The terms are: a trade discount of 20% and a cash discount of 3% for payment within 7 days.
250 pairs of socks at 45 p per pair
150 pullovers at £4·35 each
40 cricket sweaters at £8·70 each
50 assorted ties at 90 p each

12) A retailer pays £8·64 for goods after a trade discount of 25% and a cash discount of 4% have been deducted. Calculate the list price of the goods.

Summary

1) Percentages are fractions with a denominator of 100.
2) To convert a fraction into a percentage multiply it by 100.
3) To convert a percentage into a fraction divide it by 100.
4) To find the percentage of a quantity first convert the percentage into a fraction and then multiply the quantity by the fraction.

5) Profit % = $\dfrac{\text{selling price} - \text{cost price}}{\text{cost price}} \times 100$

Loss % = $\dfrac{\text{cost price} - \text{selling price}}{\text{cost price}} \times 100$

6) Mark up = $\dfrac{\text{selling price} - \text{cost price}}{\text{cost price}} \times 100$

7) Margin = $\dfrac{\text{selling price} - \text{cost price}}{\text{selling price}} \times 100$

PERCENTAGES

8) Gross profit = turnover − cost price
   Net profit = gross profit − overheads
9) Discount, which is usually a percentage of the selling price, is the amount a retailer will take off his selling price thus reducing the profit. Thus:

$$\text{Discount} = \text{selling price} \times \frac{\text{percentage discount}}{100}$$

Mental Test 9

Try to answer the following without writing anything down except the answer.

1) Express $\frac{4}{5}$ as a percentage.
2) What is 30% as a decimal fraction?
3) Express $33\frac{1}{3}$% as a vulgar fraction.
4) Convert 0·89 into a percentage.
5) What is 30% of 80?
6) What is 7% of 50?
7) What is 8% of £40?
8) If the selling price of an article is £28 and the cost price is £22, what is the profit?
9) Find the profit per cent if selling price = £25 and cost price = £20.
10) If the selling price is £30 and cost price is £40, what is the loss?
11) A car is bought for £1000 and sold for £800. What is the loss per cent?
12) An article is bought for £30. If the mark up is 20% what is the selling price?
13) Cost price = £80. Mark up = 25%. Find selling price.
14) If the selling price of an article is £50 and the cost price is £40, calculate the margin.
15) Selling price = £120. Cost price = £90. Find the margin.
16) Turnover = £40 000. Cost price = £25 000. What is the gross profit?
17) Gross profit = £22 000. Overheads = £12 000. What is the net profit?
18) Turnover = £150 000. Cost price = £100 000. Overheads = £30 000. What is the net profit?
19) A chair is offered for sale at £30. A cash discount of 5% is offered. How much is the discount?
20) A customer is offered a cash discount of 10% for prompt payment. How much will he pay for an article whose selling price is £30?

Self-Test 9

In questions 1 to 15 the answer is either true or false. State which.

1) A fraction expressed with a denominator of 100 is called a percentage.
2) $\frac{13}{25}$ is the same as 42%.
3) 0·725 is the same as 72·5%.
4) 3·5% is the same as $\frac{7}{20}$.
5) 20·45% is the same as 2·045.
6) 20% of 80 is 16.
7) If 15% of a complete length is 45 mm the complete length is 300 mm.
8) The total electorate for a certain constituency is 53 000. If 30% did not vote in an election then 37 100 did vote.
9) When a shopkeeper buys an article for £4 and sells it for £5 his percentage profit is 20%.
10) A dealer buys an article for £8 and sells it for £5. His percentage loss is 37·5%.

11) A man's salary is increased by 20% and he now gets £144 per week. Hence his salary before the increase was £120.

12) By selling an article for £9 a dealer made a profit of $33\frac{1}{3}$%. He therefore paid £6 for the article.

13) A shopkeeper marks up an article at £20 and by selling it for this price he makes a profit of 30%. On a cash sale he allows a discount of 20%. His profit on the cash sale is therefore 10%.

14) A wholesaler sells goods to a retailer at a profit of 20%. The retailer sells them to a customer at a profit of 10%. The overall profit is therefore 30%.

15) A manufacturer allows a trade discount of 25% of his list price to a retailer. In addition he allows a 5% discount for prompt payment. If the list price is £120 the retailer pays £84.

In questions 16 to 25 state the letter (or letters) which correspond to the correct answer (or answers).

16) 35% is the same as:
   a $\frac{35}{100}$ b $\frac{7}{20}$ c $\frac{35}{10}$ d 0·35

17) $\frac{11}{25}$ is the same as:
   a 4·4%   b 44%   c 22%   d 440%

18) When a dealer sells an article for £18 he makes a profit of £3. His percentage profit is therefore:
   a 20%   b $16\frac{2}{3}$%   c $14\frac{2}{7}$%   d 25%

19) When a shopkeeper buys an article for £20 and sells it for £25 his percentage profit is:
   a 20%   b 30%   c 25%   d 80%

20) A dealer buys 40 articles at a total cost of £10. He sells them at 30 p each. His percentage profit is:
   a $16\frac{2}{3}$%   b 20%   c 30%   d 25%

21) An article was sold for £60 which was a loss on the cost price of 10%. The cost price was therefore:
   a £54   b £66
   c £66·66   d £70·50

22) The duty on an article is 25% of its value. If the duty paid is 80 p the value of the article is:
   a £8   b £3·20   c £1·80   d £1

23) An article is offered for sale at £120 which represents a mark up of 20%. On a cash sale he allows a discount of 10%. His profit on the sale is therefore:
   a 10%   b 8%   c 30%   d 18%

24) 30% of a certain length is 600 mm. The complete length is:
   a 20 mm   b 200 mm
   c 2000 mm   d 2 m

25) When a shopkeeper sells articles for £37·80 each he makes a profit of 26% on the cost price. During a sale the articles are marked at £31·20 each. He therefore makes a profit of:
   a 31%   b 3·8%   c 5%   d 4%

10. Statistics

UNDERSTAND THE USE OF THE AVERAGE IN BUSINESS
    Calculate the arithmetic mean.
    Identify the median and mode in an array.
    Identify the uses of arithmetic mean, median and mode.
UNDERSTAND THE USE OF PROPER VISUAL PRESENTATION TO BUSINESS DATA
    Construct appropriate charts and diagrams from given data.
    Interpret the charts and graphs as above.

Statistical Averages

There are three statistical averages which are in common use. They are the arithmetic mean, the median and the mode.

The arithmetic mean. This is the commonest statistical average and it is determined by adding up all the quantities in a set of quantities and dividing by the number of quantities in the set. Thus:

$$\text{arithmetic mean} = \frac{\text{sum of the quantities}}{\text{no. of quantities}}$$

Example 1   The wages of 6 people working in an office are: £46·93, £54·65, £47·69, £85·00, £94·50 and £73·95. Calculate the mean wage.

$$\text{Mean wage} = \frac{46·93 + 54·65 + 47·69 + 85·00 + 94·50 + 73·95}{6}$$

$$= \frac{402·72}{6} = £67·12$$

Example 2   In a small factory, 5 people earn a wage of £72 each, 3 earn a wage of £80 each and 2 earn a wage of £84 each. Calculate the mean wage for the office.

    Total wages of 5 people at £72 each = 5 × £72 = £360
    Total wages of 3 people at £80 each = 3 × £80 = £240
    Total wages of 2 people at £84 each = 2 × £84 = £168
    Total wages of 10 people   = £768

$$\text{Mean wage} = \frac{£768}{10} = £76·80$$

Example 3   An industrial organisation gives an aptitude test to all applicants for employment. The results of 150 people taking the test was as follows:

Score (out of 10)	1	2	3	4	5	6	7	8	9	10
No. of applicants	6	12	15	21	35	24	20	10	6	1

What was the average score obtained by all the applicants?

Total score = 1×6+2×12+3×15+4×21+5×35+6×24+7×20+8×10+9×6+10×1 = 762

Total number of applicants = 150

Mean score = $\dfrac{\text{total mark}}{\text{no. of applicants}} = \dfrac{762}{150} = 5\cdot08$

The median. If a set of quantities is arranged in ascending (or descending) order of size, the median is the value which is half-way along the set. Thus the median of 3, 5, 7, 8, 10 is 7. If the number of quantities in the set is even then the median is the average of the two middle values. Thus the median of 2, 3, 5, 7, 8, 9 is $\frac{1}{2}\times(5+7) = \frac{1}{2}\times 12 = 6$.

Example 4

The wages of 7 people working in an office are £1·20, £1·08, £0·75, £2·49, £1·36, £0·67 and £1·98 per hour. What is the median wage?

The first step is to arrange the wages in ascending order.

0·67 0·75 1·08 1·20 1·36 1·98 2·49

The median is now the middle value which is 1·20. Hence the median wage is £1·20.

Example 5

The heights of 8 students at a college were as follows: 177·8, 162·6, 167·6, 182·0, 165·3, 157·5, 185·4 and 169·8 cm. Find the median height.

Arranging the heights in ascending order of size we have:

157·5 162·6 165·3 167·6 169·8 177·8 182·0 185·4

The two middle values are 167·6 and 169·8 and hence the median height is $\frac{1}{2}\times(167\cdot6+169\cdot8) = \frac{1}{2}\times 337\cdot4 = 168\cdot7$ cm.

The mode. The quantity which occurs most frequently in a set of quantities is called the mode. Thus the mode of the set of numbers 20, 22, 25, 25, 27, 27, 27, 30, 30, 31, 33 and 35 is 27 since this number occurs three times which is more than any of the other numbers.

Example 6

In an aptitude test 12 candidates obtained the following scores out of 20. 3, 4, 4, 7, 7, 8, 9, 9, 9, 12, 12, 15. Find the mode.

Three of the candidates scored 9 marks which is the most frequently occurring mark. Hence the mode is 9 marks.

The arithmetic mean takes into account extreme values which may not be truly representative of the group as a whole. The median and the mode avoid this and in many cases will give a better average than the arithmetic mean. The median can often be located with greater accuracy than the mode because there may be more than one mode in a set of quantities. However the mode is useful for such things as stock sizes. It is not much good if a manufacturer of men's trousers finds that the mean length of men's legs is 81·28 cm since this may not be a stock size. What he wants to know is which stock size is the most popular and the mode will give him this information.

STATISTICS

Exercise 59

1) Find the mean of the following measurements: 22·3 mm, 22·5 mm, 22·6 mm, 21·8 mm and 22·0 mm.

2) Find the mean of 95 kg, 128 kg, 38 kg, 97 kg, and 217 kg.

3) In a small office 5 people earn a wage per week of £108 each, 3 earn a wage of £120 each and 2 earn a wage of £126 each. Calculate the mean wage.

4) 12 metal castings weigh 12 kg each and 8 similar castings weigh 12·5 kg each. Find the mean weight of the 20 castings.

5) The marks of a student in 4 examinations were: 84, 90, 72 and 62. Find the mean mark.

6) The wages of 60 employees in a company were as follows:

Wage £	80	81	82	83	84	85	86
Number of employees	7	9	16	13	9	5	1

Calculate the mean wage.

7) The marks of 50 students taking a test were as follows (marks out of 20):

Mark	12	13	14	15	16	17	18
Number of students	3	8	11	18	7	2	1

Find the mean mark.

8) Find the arithmetic mean of the following:

Length (cm)	29·5	29·6	29·7	29·8	29·9	30·0	30·1	30·2
Number of lengths	3	7	22	28	18	12	7	3

9) The rainfall in millimetres falling on a town on 5 successive days was as follows: 23, 28, 13, 42, 17. Find the median.

10) The wages of 8 people working on a small section of a factory are as follows: £1·89, £2·06, £1·75, £2·48, £1·63, £2·08, £1·97, £1·42. Find the median wage.

11) Find the median of the following sets of numbers:
 (a) 2, 3, 3, 5, 6, 7, 8
 (b) 4, 4, 6, 8, 9, 11, 14, 16
 (c) 8, 9, 8, 7, 9, 6, 10, 7, 9

12) The figures below represent the daily output of a factory on 14 successive working days:
27, 42, 35, 63, 38, 75, 63, 72, 75, 61, 63, 65, 63, 75
Find the median and the mode.

13) Find the mode of the following set of numbers:
2, 8, 11, 3, 7, 8, 11, 12, 8, 15, 9, 8, 11, 8, 6, 4, 10, 2

14) Find the mean, median and mode for the numbers 26, 36, 24, 22, 26, 38, 22, 32 and 22.

Charts and Graphs

In newspapers, business reports and government publications use is made of pictorial illustrations to present and compare quantities of the same kind. These diagrams help the reader to understand what deductions can be drawn from the quantities represented. The most common forms are charts and graphs.

Axes of Reference

To plot a graph we first take two lines at right angles to each other (Fig. 10.1). These lines are called the axes of reference. Their intersection, the point O, is called the origin. The vertical axis is often called the y-axis and the horizontal axis is then called the x-axis.

Fig. 10.1

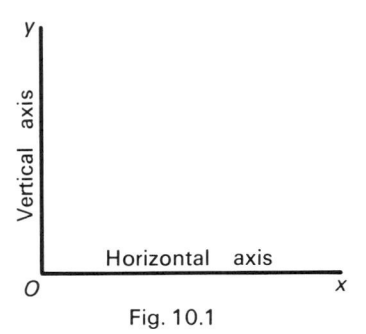

Scales

The number of units represented by a unit length along an axis is called the scale on that axis. For instance 1 cm could represent 2 units. The scale is determined from the highest and lowest values to be plotted along an axis. It should be as large as possible but it must also be chosen so that it is easy to read. The scales need not be the same on both axes. The most useful scales are 1, 2 and 5 units to 1 large square on the graph paper. Some multiples of these such as 10, 20, 100 units, etc. to 1 large square are also suitable.

Coordinates

Coordinates are used to mark the points of a graph. In Fig. 10.2, values of x are to be plotted against values of y. The point P has been plotted so that $x = 8$ and $y = 10$. The values of 8 and 10 are said to be the rectangular coordinates of the point P.

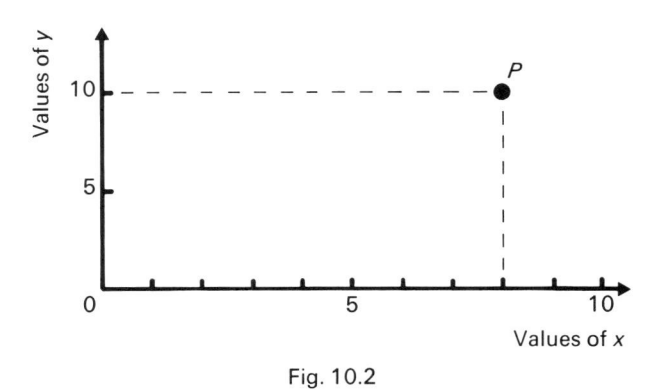

Fig. 10.2

Drawing a Graph

Every graph shows a relation between two sets of numbers. The table below gives the average diameter of ash trees of varying ages.

Age in years	5	10	15	20	25	30	40	50	70
Diameter (cm)	7·6	9·3	12·2	16·2	21·4	27·7	43·8	64·5	119·7

To plot the graph we first draw the two axes of reference (Fig. 10.3). We then choose suitable scales to represent the age in years along the horizontal axis and the diameter along the vertical axis. Scales of 1 cm = 10 years (horizontally) and 1 cm = 20 cm (vertically) have been chosen. On plotting the graph we see that it is a smooth curve which passes through all of the plotted points.

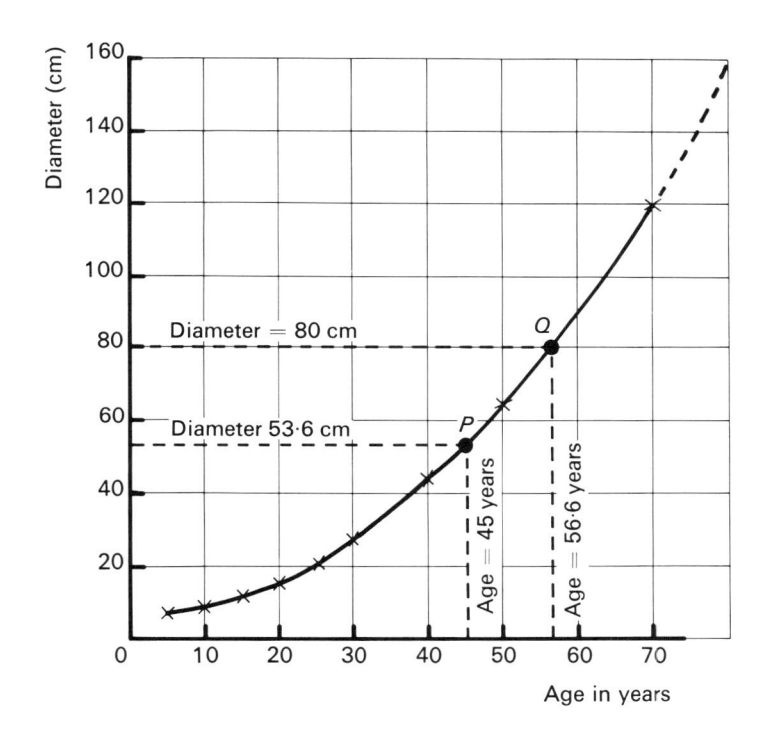

Fig. 10.3

When a graph is either a smooth curve or a straight line we can use the graph to deduce corresponding values not given in the table of values. Thus to find the diameter of a tree which is 45 years old we first find 45 on the horizontal axis and from this point we draw a vertical line to meet the curve at P. From P we now draw a horizontal line to the vertical axis and read off the value. It is found to be 53·6. Hence a tree which is 45 years old will have a diameter of 53·6 cm.

Suppose now that we wish to know the age of a tree with a diameter of 80 cm. We find 80 cm on the vertical axis and from this point we draw a horizontal line to meet the curve at Q. From Q we draw a vertical line to the horizontal axis and read off the value. It is found to be 56·6. Hence a tree with a diameter of 80 cm is 56·6 years old.

Using a graph in this way to find values which are not given in the table is called *interpolation*. If we extend the curve so that it follows the general trend we can estimate values of the diameter and age which lie just beyond the range of the given values. Thus in Fig. 10.3 by extending the curve we can find the probable diameter of a tree which is 75 years old. This is found to be 136·4 cm.

Finding a value in this way is called *extrapolation*. An extrapolated value can usually be relied upon, but in certain cases it may contain a substantial amount of error. Extrapolated values must therefore be used with care. It must be clearly understood that interpolation can only be used if the graph is a smooth curve or a straight line. It is no good applying interpolation to the graph of Example 7.

Example 7 The table below gives the temperature at 12.00 noon on seven successive days. Plot a graph to illustrate this information with the day horizontal.

Day June	1	2	3	4	5	6	7
Temp. °C	16	20	16	18	22	15	16·5

As before we draw two axes at right-angles to each other, indicating the day on the horizontal axis. Since the temperatures range from 15° to 22°C we can make 14°C (say) our starting point on the vertical axis. This will allow us to use a larger scale on that axis which makes for greater accuracy in plotting the graph.

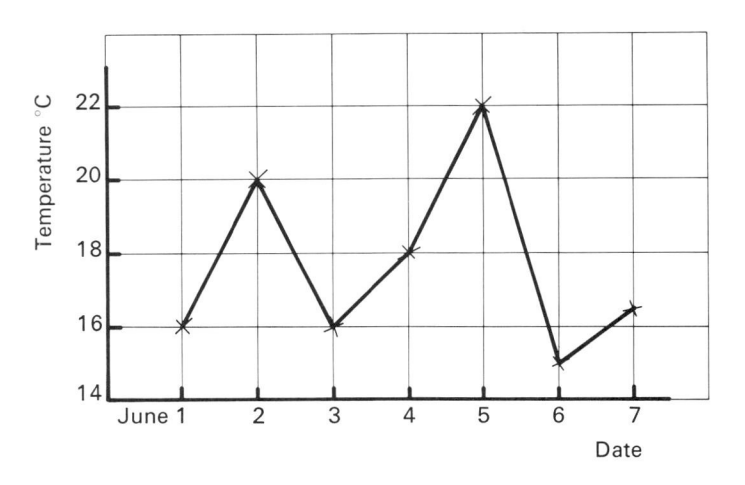

Fig. 10.4

On plotting the points (Fig. 10.4) we see that it is impossible to join the points by means of a smooth curve. The best we can do is to join the points by means of a series of straight lines. The graph then presents in pictorial form the variations in temperature and we can see at a glance that the 1st, 3rd and 6th June were cool days whilst the 2nd and 5th were warm days.

STATISTICS

Exercise 60

1) The table below shows the amount of steel delivered to a factory during five successive weeks. Plot a graph to show this with the number of weeks on the horizontal axis.

Week number	1	2	3
Amount delivered (kg)	25 000	65 000	80 000

Week number	4	5
Amount delivered (kg)	30 000	50 000

2) The areas of circles for various diameters is shown in the table below. Plot a graph with the diameter on the horizontal axis and from it estimate the area of a circle whose diameter is 18 cm.

Diameter (cm)	5	10	15	20	25
Area (cm²)	19·6	78·5	177·6	314·2	492·2

3) The output of a factory in 8 successive weeks is given in the table below. Plot a graph to show this with the number of weeks on the horizontal axis.

Week number	1	2	3	4	5	6	7	8
Output (units)	83	65	78	89	96	88	73	69

4) The table below gives the amounts for £1 invested at 8% interest per annum for the periods stated.

Years	2	4	6	8	10	12	14
Amounts in £	1·17	1·36	1·59	1·85	2·16	2·52	2·94

Plot the years horizontally and find the amount after 7 years.

5) Two quantities W and P are connected as shown by the following table of values:

W	28	50	59	67	74	79	84
P	2·0	5·4	6·8	8·0	9·1	9·9	10·6

Plot a graph with P plotted horizontally and find the value of W when $P = 7·4$. What is the value of P when $W = 77$?

The Pie Chart

Suppose that in a factory the number of persons employed on various jobs is as shown in the following table:

Type of personnel	Number employed
Unskilled workers	45
Craftsmen	25
Draughtsmen	5
Clerical staff	10
Total	85

The pie charts displays the information as angles, the size of the angle being proportional to the number employed. It will be remembered that there are 360° in a circle. Hence for unskilled workers the angle is $\frac{45}{85} \times 360° = 190°$ and for craftsmen the angle is $\frac{25}{85} \times 360° = 106°$, etc.

The resulting pie chart is shown in Fig. 10.5.

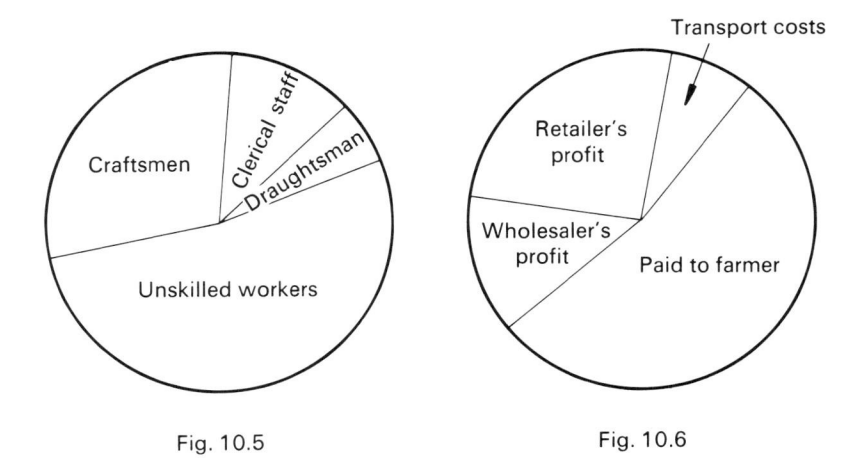

Fig. 10.5

Fig. 10.6

Example 8 An analysis of the cost of potatoes retailed at 15 p per kilogram was as follows:

Paid to farmer	8 p per kilogram
Wholesaler's profit	2 p
Retailer's profit	4 p
Transport costs	1 p

Represent this information on a pie chart.

Item	Pence	Centre angle
Paid to farmer	8	$\frac{8}{15} \times 360° = 192°$
Wholesaler's profit	2	$\frac{2}{15} \times 360° = 48°$
Retailer's profit	4	$\frac{4}{15} \times 360° = 96°$
Transport costs	1	$\frac{1}{15} \times 360° = 24°$
Totals	15	360°

The pie chart is shown in Fig. 10.6.

The Proportionate Bar Chart

This diagram relies upon heights (or areas) to convey the proportions, the total height of the diagram representing the total or 100%.

STATISTICS

Example 9   Represent the information given in Example 8 in the form of a bar chart.

Item	Pence	Percentage
Paid to farmer	8	$\frac{8}{15} \times 100 = 53\%$
Wholesaler's profit	2	$\frac{2}{15} \times 100 = 13\%$
Retailer's profit	4	$\frac{4}{15} \times 100 = 27\%$
Transport costs	1	$\frac{1}{15} \times 100 = 7\%$
Totals	15	100%

The bar chart is shown in Fig. 10.7.

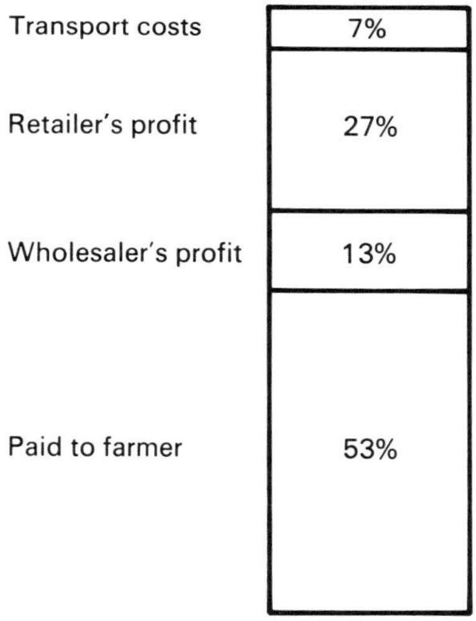

Fig. 10.7

The Horizontal Bar Chart

This gives a better comparison of the costs involved (see Example 8) but it does not readily display the total costs.

Example 10   Draw a horizontal bar chart for the information given in Example 8. The diagram is shown in Fig. 10.8.

Fig. 10.8

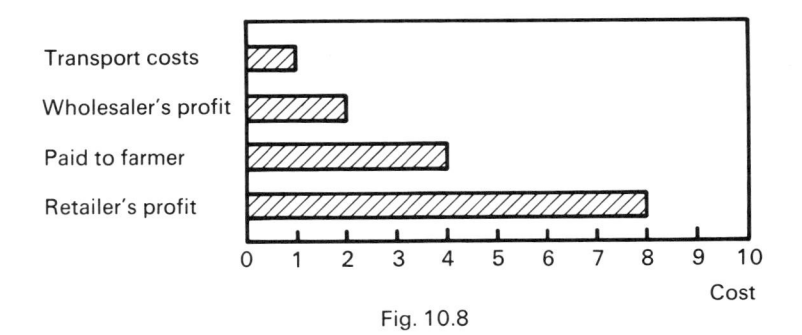

The Vertical Bar Chart

This is sometimes used instead of a horizontal bar chart (see Fig. 10.9).

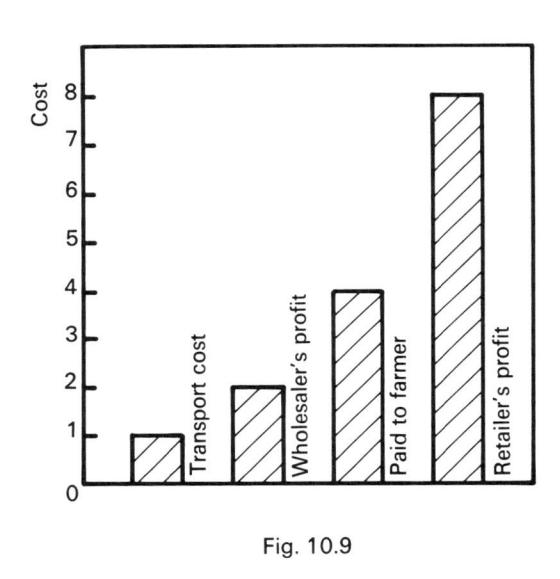

Fig. 10.9

Representing Information on Pictograms

Pictures are often used to represent information and when these are used the resulting diagram is called a pictogram.

Example 11 The table below shows the output of bicycles for the years 1970 to 1974.

Year	1970	1971	1972	1973	1974
Output	2000	4000	7000	8500	9000

Represent this data in the form of a pictogram.

The pictogram is shown in Fig. 10.10 and it will be seen that each bicycle represents an output of 2000 bicycles. Part of a symbol as shown in 1972, 1973 and 1974 is used to represent a fraction of 2000 but only a very approximate idea of true value can be given by doing this.

STATISTICS

[Pictogram: bicycles by year, 1970–1974]

1970 — 1 bicycle
1971 — 2 bicycles
1972 — 3½ bicycles
1973 — 4½ bicycles
1974 — 4½ bicycles

🚲 = 2000 bicycles

Fig. 10.10

A bar chart provides a more accurate way of presenting information than does a pictogram.

Example 12 The table shows the output of motor-cycles by Richards & Co. for the years 1970 to 1976 inclusive. Represent this information in the form of a vertical bar chart.

Year	1970	1971	1972	1973	1974	1975	1976
Output	8000	7300	6200	5600	5700	5400	5900

The bar chart is shown in Fig. 10.11.

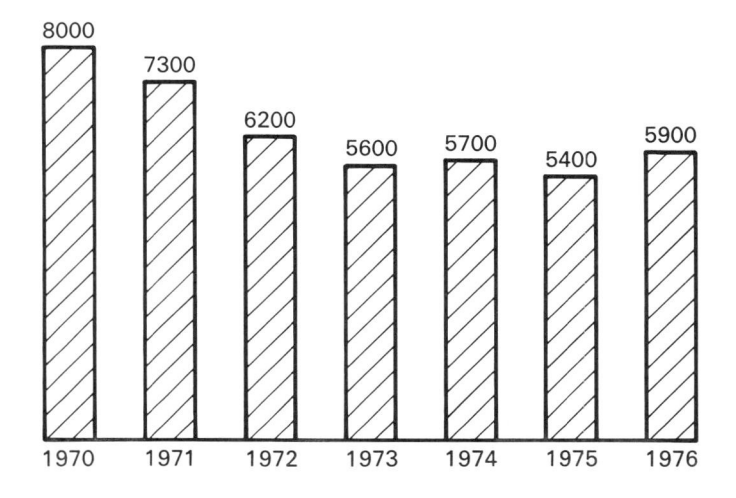

Fig. 10.11

Exercise 61

1) A building contractor surveying his labour force finds that 35% are engaged on factories, 40% are engaged on house building and 25% are engaged on public works (schools, hospitals, etc.).
   (a) Draw a pie chart of this information.
   (b) Present the information in the form of a single bar chart.

2) A firm finds that each pound received from sales is spent in the following way:

Raw materials	£0·38
Wages and salaries	£0·29
Machinery etc.	£0·08
Advertising etc.	£0·15
Profit	£0·10

Construct a pie chart of this information.

3) A department store has monthly takings of £40 000. It is divided between the various departments as follows:

Men's clothing	£10 000
Women's clothing	£15 000
Hardware	£ 5 000
Electrical	£ 8 000
Stationery	£ 2 000

Draw a pie chart of this information.

4) Draw a horizontal bar chart for the information given in Question 3.

5) In a certain factory the number of personnel employed on various jobs as follows: Machinists 140, Fitters 120, Clerical staff 80, Labourers 10, Draughtsmen 20. Represent this information:
   (a) in a pie chart,
   (b) in a single bar chart,
   (c) in a horizontal bar chart.

6) A department store has monthly takings of £40 000. It is divided between the various departments as follows:

Men's clothing	£10 000
Women's clothing	£15 000
Hardware	£5 000
Electrical	£8 000
Stationery	£2 000

Draw, to represent this data,
   (a) a vertical bar chart,
   (b) a horizontal bar chart.

7) The figures below relate to the value of exports to various trade areas in 1965.

Area	Value of exports (£ millions)
E.E.C.	78
E.F.T.A.	52
Commonwealth	110
U.S.A.	35
Latin America	12
Soviet block	5
Others	82

Draw a vertical bar chart to represent this information.

8) The annual sales of motor cars by Mortimer & Co. were as follows:

Year	1972	1973	1974	1975	1976
Sales	2000	2500	3200	2700	3000

Represent this data,
   (a) on a pictogram,
   (b) on a vertical bar chart.

9) The table below gives the number of houses completed in the S.W. area of England, in various years.

Year	1965	1969	1969	1971	1973
Number of houses completed (thousands)	81	69	73	84	80

Represent this information by means of a pictogram.

10) The information given below shows the production of tyres by the Treadwell Tyre Company for the first six months of the year 1963.

Month	Jan.	Feb.	March	April	May	June
Production (thousands)	40	43	39	38	37	45

Represent this information in the form of a pictogram and in the form of a vertical bar chart.

STATISTICS

Interpreting Charts and Diagrams

The proportionate bar chart and the pie chart both have the disadvantage in that it is difficult to make mental comparisons between the component parts of the chart. However, in interpreting these charts it is possible to gain some idea of the quantities represented.

Example 13 Fig. 10.12 is a proportionate bar chart which shows the amounts of various chemicals used by a certain factory in one month. From the chart, estimate the amounts of each chemical given that the total amount used is 12 000 tonnes.

Potassium nitrate

Copper sulphate

Nitric acid

Sulphuric acid

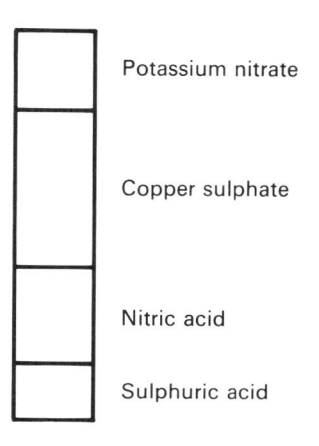

Fig. 10.12

By using a rule the total height of the chart is found to be 10 cm. The heights for sulphuric acid, nitric acid, copper sulphate and potassium nitrate are 1·5 cm, 2·5 cm, 4·0 cm and 2·0 cm respectively.

Hence,
    10 cm represents 12 000 tonnes
    1·0 cm represents $\frac{12\,000}{10}$ = 1200 tonnes
    1·5 cm represents 1200 × 1·5 = 1800 tonnes
    2·5 cm represents 1200 × 2·5 = 3000 tonnes
    4·0 cm represents 1200 × 4·0 = 4800 tonnes
    2·0 cm represents 1200 × 2·0 = 2400 tonnes

The amounts of each chemical used are, therefore, 1800 t of sulphuric acid, 3000 t of nitric acid, 4800 t of copper sulphate and 2400 t of potassium nitrate.

Example 14 Fig. 10.13 is a pie chart showing the way in which each pound of income was spent in 1968. Find the actual amounts spent on the various items per pound of income.

Using a protractor the sector angles are found to be: food and drink 130°, housing 60°, transport 40°, clothing 50° and other 80°. Since there are 360° in a circle the amounts spent on the various items are:

Fig. 10.13

$$\text{Food and drink } \frac{130}{360} \times £1 = 36\,\text{p}$$

$$\text{Housing } \frac{60}{360} \times £1 = 17\,\text{p}$$

$$\text{Transport } \frac{40}{360} \times £1 = 11\,\text{p}$$

$$\text{Clothing } \frac{50}{360} \times £1 = 14\,\text{p}$$

$$\text{Other } \frac{80}{360} \times £1 = 22\,\text{p}$$

Bar charts, both horizontal and vertical, usually possess a scale and hence they are easy to read.

Example 15 Fig. 10.14 is a vertical bar chart which shows the number of people purchasing clothing on five days of a certain week. Write down these numbers.

In order to find the required numbers we have to estimate the height of each bar. These are found to be: Monday 100, Tuesday 170, Wednesday 125, Thursday 200 and Friday 225.

Great care is needed in interpreting graphs which can sometimes be misleading. Some of the pitfalls are as follows:

(i) Zero line not shown thus creating a false impression of the heights of the graph (see Fig. 10.15).

(ii) Scales not shown thereby making it difficult to see the magnitudes of the quantities represented.

(iii) The steepness of a graph represents the rate of increase (or decrease). By manipulating the scales an erroneous impression can easily be created (see Fig. 10.16).

STATISTICS

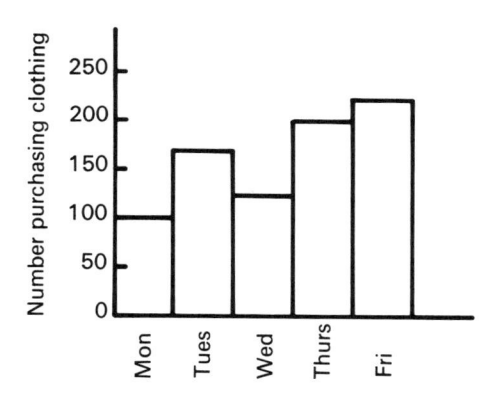

Fig. 10.14

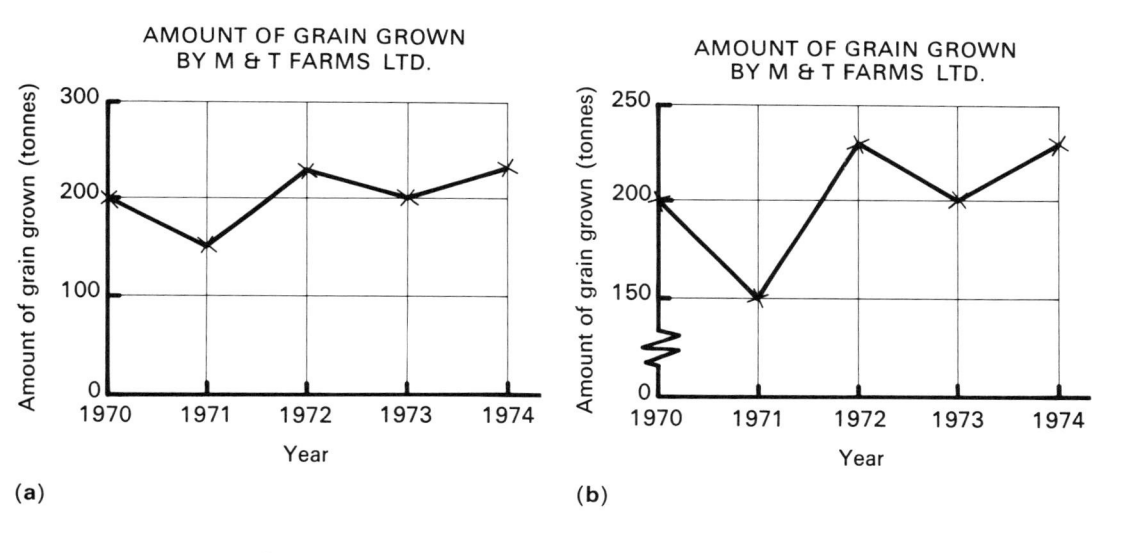

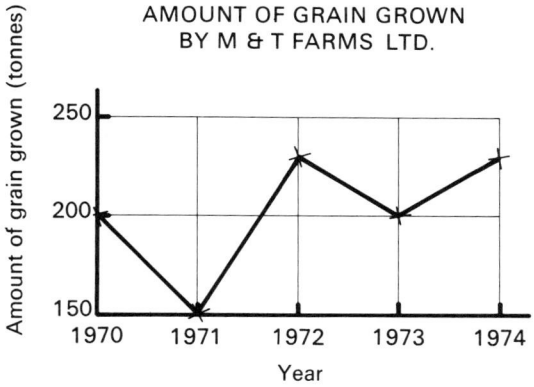

AMOUNT OF GRAIN GROWN
BY M & T FARMS LTD.

(a)

AMOUNT OF GRAIN GROWN
BY M & T FARMS LTD.

(b)

AMOUNT OF GRAIN GROWN
BY M & T FARMS LTD.

(c)

Fig. 10.15

Example 16 The figures below show the amount of grain grown by M & T Farms Ltd. in the years 1970 to 1974. Draw a graph to represent this information.

Year	1970	1971	1972	1973	1974
Amount grown (tonnes)	200	150	230	200	230

If we draw the graph as shown in Fig. 10.15(a) a considerable amount of graph paper is wasted. Fig. 10.15(b) shows a method of avoiding this waste of paper and allowing a much larger vertical scale to be used. Note that zero is shown at the bottom of the scale and that a definite break in the scale has been shown. The method used in Fig. 10.15(c) must *never* be used because zero is not shown.

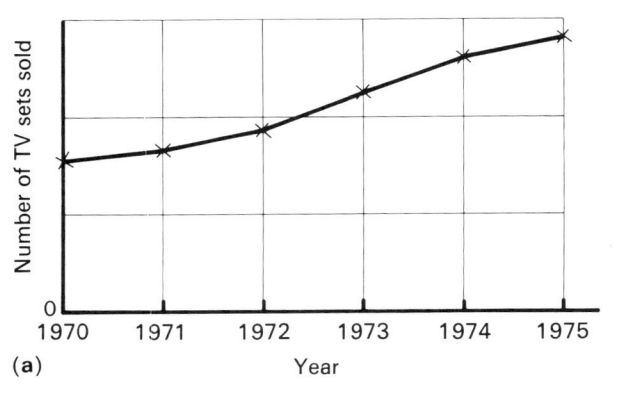

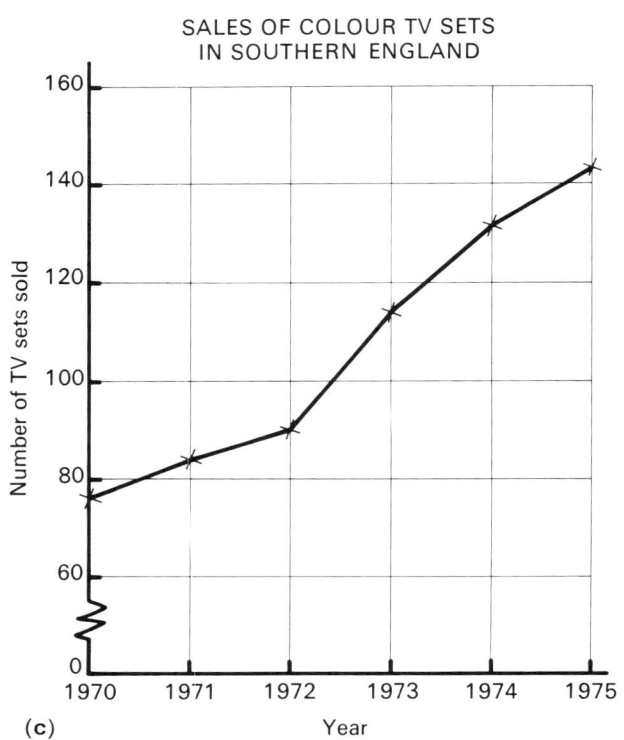

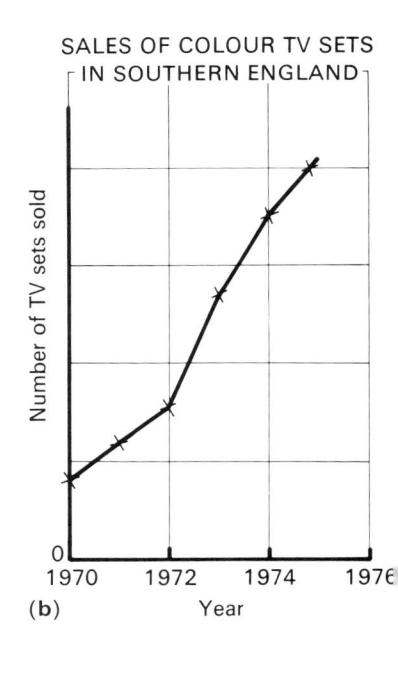

Fig. 10.16

STATISTICS

Example 17 The table below shows the number of colour TV sets sold in Southern England during the years 1970 to 1975. Represent this data on a suitable graph.

Year	1970	1971	1972	1973	1974	1975
Number sold (thousands)	77	84	91	115	131	143

In Fig. 10.16(a) a small vertical scale has been chosen and it appears that sales are increasing very slowly. In Fig. 10.16(b) the vertical scale has been made large compared to the horizontal scale. It gives the impression that sales are increasing very rapidly. These impressions are heightened by the fact that no vertical scale is given. Figure 10.16(c) gives the correct impression.

Note that in both Figs. 10.15 and 10.16 the points on the graph have been joined by straight lines. This is because no information is given regarding intermediate periods (e.g. monthly sales).

Exercise 62

1) The table below shows the number of housing grants granted to local authorities, private owners and housing associations for the years 1961 to 1971. Draw a suitable graph of this information plotting the years on the horizontal axis.

Year	1961	1966	1969	1970	1971
Number of grants	134	117	126	183	236

2) The table below gives the sales during the first six months of 1976 by a trading firm. Plotting months on the horizontal axis, draw a graph of this data.

Month	Jan.	Feb.	March	April	May	June
Sales (£ thousands)	27	24	22	42	44	56

3) The table below shows the advertising expenditure by a firm during the last six months of 1977. Draw a graph of this information, plotting the months on the horizontal axis.

Month	July	Aug.	Sept.	Oct.	Nov.	Dec.
Expenditure (£ thousands)	26	52	11	47	51	36

4) The table below gives the total number of road casualties in the years 1968 to 1974. Plotting years along the horizontal axis, draw a graph to illustrate this information.

Year	1968	1969	1970	1971	1972	1973	1974
Casualties (thousands)	88	90	94	91	91	89	93

5) Figure 10.17 is a diagram representing the total amounts of various fruits grown on a fruit farm. The total amount of fruit grown is 80 tonnes. Estimate the amounts of each fruit grown.

6) Figure 10.18 is a vertical bar chart which shows the number of items sold in 7 successive weeks.

(a) Write down the number of items sold in each of the 7 weeks.
(b) Find the total number of items sold in the first 3 weeks.

7) Figure 10.19 is a horizontal bar chart which shows the number of votes cast for the various parties in a General Election. Write down the number of votes cast for each party.

8) Figure 10.20 shows the production of a steel mill for the years 1973 to 1977. Find the amount of production in the years 1973 and 1976. How much was the total amount of steel produced during all the years depicted?

9) Figure 10.21 shows the total sales of a departmental store in one week when the total sales were £20 000. Estimate the sales for each department.

10) The pie chart shown in Fig. 10.22 shows absences from school for various reasons. There were 60 children absent altogether. How many children had 'flu? How many were on holiday with their parents? How many were late or had no reason for being absent?

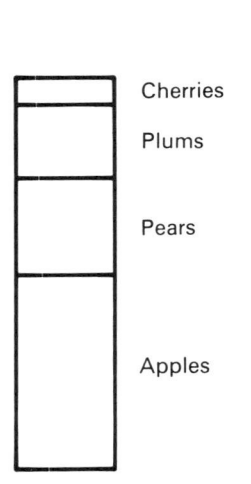

Fig. 10.17

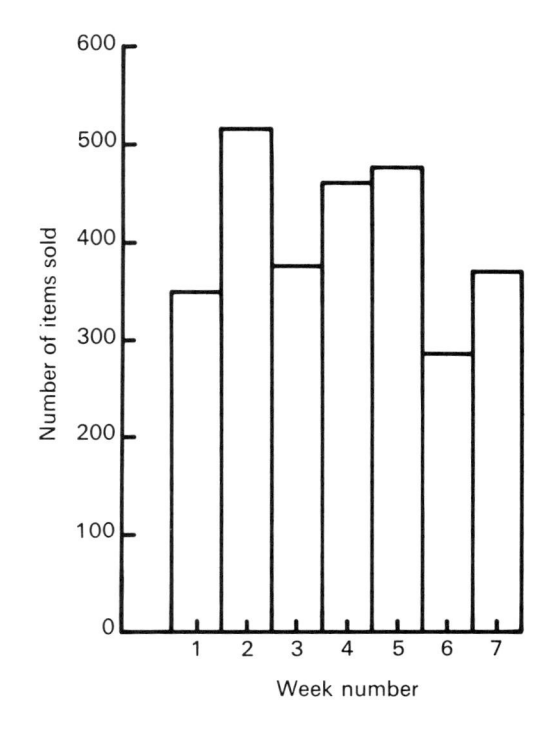

Fig. 10.18

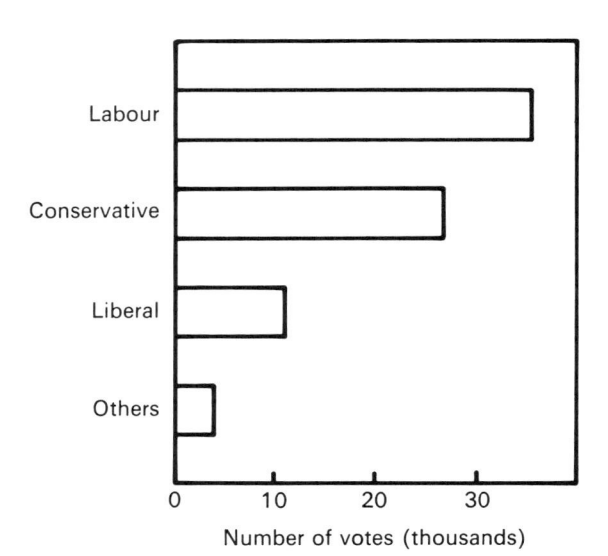

Fig. 10.19

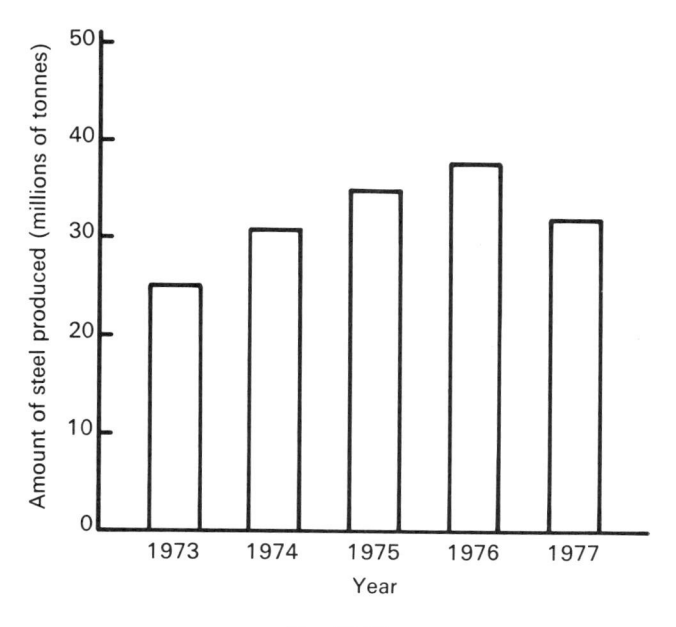

Fig. 10.20

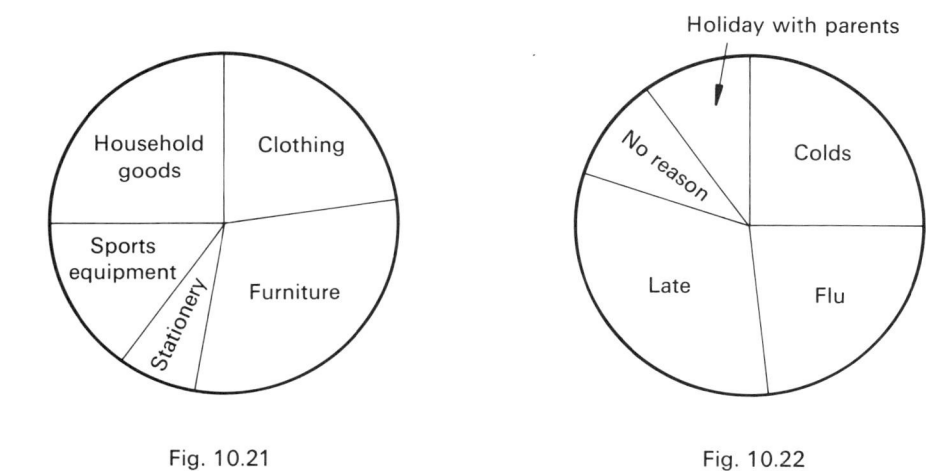

Fig. 10.21

Fig. 10.22

Summary

1) Arithmetic mean $= \dfrac{\text{sum of the quantities}}{\text{no. of quantities}}$.

2) When a set of quantities is arranged in ascending (or descending) order of size the median is the middle value of the set. If the set contains an even number of quantities then the median value is the average of the two middle values.

3) The mode is the value which occurs most frequently in a set of quantities.

4) Coordinates are used to mark the points on a graph. When a graph is either a smooth curve or a straight line we can use the graph to deduce values not given in the table from which the graph was drawn. Using a graph in this way is called interpolation.

5) If we extend a graph so that it follows the general trend we can find values which are outside of the range of values given. Using a graph in this way is called extrapolation.

6) Pie charts are used to represent the relative sizes of a number of quantities. The angle at the centre is proportional to the size of the quantity represented.

7) A proportional bar chart relies upon heights (or areas) to represent the proportions of the quantities represented. The total height of the diagram is equal to the total of the quantities.

8) The horizontal and vertical bar charts represents each of the quantities given but it does not readily display the total of the quantities.

Self-Test 10

1) For the numbers 13, 18, 12, 11, 13, 19, 11, 16 and 11, the number 13 is:

   a the mean   **b** the median
   c the mode   **d** none of these

2) What is the median of the numbers 4, 12, 6, 6, 8, 14 and 20?

   a 6   **b** 8   **c** 10   **d** 70

3) The mean of the numbers 1, 8, 7, 6, 6, 1, 3, 6, 5, 2 is:

   a 5   **b** 4·5   **c** 10   **d** 5·5

4) The pie chart (Fig. 10.23) shows the output of items from five factories A, B, C, D, and E, The correct size of the sector angle for factory C is:

   a 15°   **b** 24°   **c** 30°   **d** 54°
   e 108°

5) The chart (Fig. 10.24) shows the number of learner drivers who failed to pass their test with different examiners on a certain day. How many of them passed their test that day?

   a 9   **b** 10   **c** 15   **d** 25   **e** 40

6) The diagram (Fig. 10.25) shows the attendance of a class each day for a school week. The mean daily attendance was:

   a 34   **b** 28   **c** 30   **d** 29

7) The pie chart (Fig. 10.26) represents the votes cast by 72 000 people in a certain town. The percentage who voted Liberal was:

   a 2·1%   **b** 21%   **c** 75%   **d** 7·5%

8) In Fig. 10.26 the number who voted Labour was about:

   a 36 000   **b** 15 800   **c** 32 000
   d none of these

9) In a football league of 24 teams the following frequency table shows the number of goals scored in the league matches played on one Saturday afternoon.

Number of goals scored	0	1	2	3	4
Number of teams	5	8	4	2	1

The mean number of goals scored was:

   a 1   **b** 0·83   **c** 1·5   **d** 1·3
   e 1·08

10) If the information in question 9 was shown on a pie chart, the sector angle representing 3 goals would be:

   a 90°   **b** 36°   **c** 144°   **d** 60°
   e 72°

STATISTICS

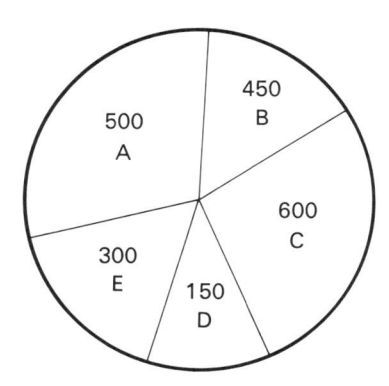

Fig. 10.23 (not to scale)

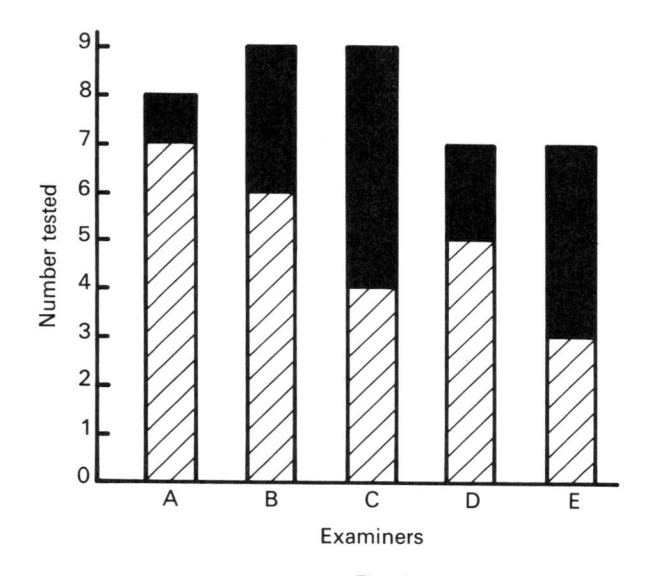

Fig. 10.24

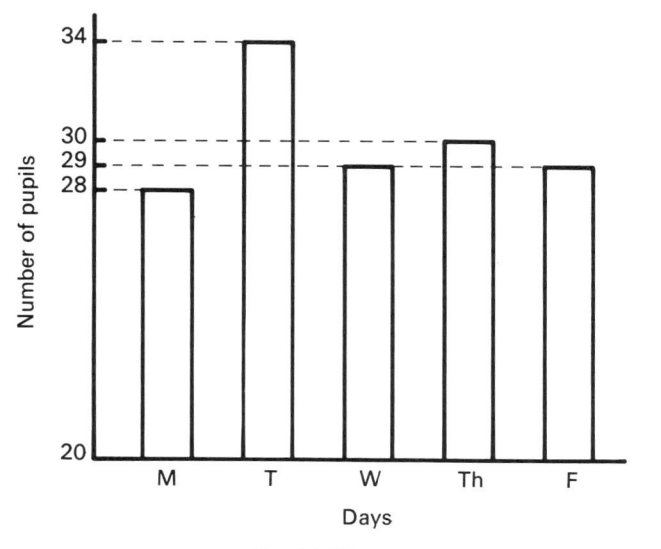

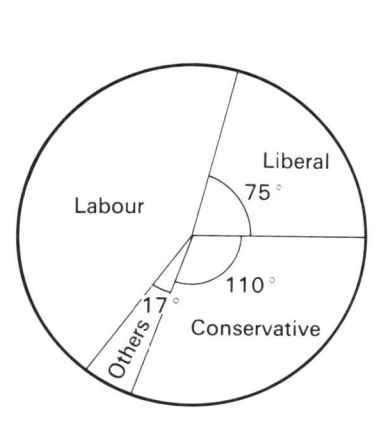

Fig. 10.25

Fig. 10.26

Revision Questions

1) (a) Subtract 8 km 900 m from 11 km 450 m.
   (b) Taking 8 kilometres as equal to 5 miles, how far is $35\frac{3}{4}$ miles in kilometres?
   (c) If 2·54 cm = 1 inch, find the dimensions in centimetres of a page measuring 5 inches by $7\frac{1}{2}$ inches.
   (d) If 1 litre = 1·76 pints, express 3 gallons in litres to the nearest litre.

2) (a) Divide 24 by 0·005.
   (b) Find 7 per cent of £40.
   (c) Express 25 seconds as a fraction of an hour, in its lowest terms.

3) (a) Express $\frac{7}{9}$ as a decimal correct to 2 places.
   (b) A man earns £3,900 per year. How much per week is this?
   (c) Find the value of $3\frac{3}{8} \div \frac{27}{56}$.
   (d) Reduce $\frac{121}{187}$ to its lowest terms.

4) Find the exact value of:
   (a) 3·9865 × 0·875   (b) 245·81 ÷ 4·7

5) Find, to 2 decimal places:
   (a) The height in inches of a barometer which stands at 772·1 mm.
   (b) The height in mm of a barometer which stands at 30·71 inches. (Given 1 metre = 39·37 inches.)

6) Use 'practice' or 'short methods' to calculate the following:
   (a) 3 metres 33 centimetres at £1·45 per metre,
   (b) 78 kilograms 55 grams at £30 per kilogram,
   (c) 1014 articles at £1·36 each.
Answers to the nearest pence.

7) (a) A motor car tank's capacity is 22 gallons of petrol. How much is this in litres? (Note: 1 litre = 1·76 pints.)
   (b) A road journey is 80 miles. How much is this in kilometres? (Note: 1 kilometre = $\frac{5}{8}$ of a mile.)

8) Betasprings Ltd. has an annual production of 9600 units, spread evenly through the year. There is no opening stock at 1st January. The sales are as follows:

January	600	May	400	September	800
February	500	June	800	October	700
March	300	July	1200	November	800
April	900	August	1100	December	500

Show these statistics by means of a bar graph.

9) Copy the following table and complete it by calculating and filling in the missing figures:

Gross Costs £1000	Trade Discount (20%) £	Cash Discount (5%) £	Net amount payable £
200	(10%) £	NIL £	£
800	(25%) £	(5%) £	£
250	NIL £	(10%) £	£
Totals £	XXX £	XXX £	£

10) Show by means of a line or bar graph, the comparative sales of departments A, B and C, as shown below.

£ (thousands)

	Department A	Department B	Department C
January	18	40	38
February	14	32	36
March	20	30	32
April	26	30	40
May	30	24	30
June	35	22	32

11) Find the exact values of each of the following:
   (a) $\dfrac{13^2 \times 11^2}{26}$
   (b) $\dfrac{13^3 \times 11^3}{22}$
   (c) 4069 × 15

12) The list price of an article is £800.
   (a) How much will the customer pay if trade discount is 25% and cash discount is 5%?
   (b) How much will he pay if trade discount is reduced to 20% and cash discount is raised to 10%?

REVISION QUESTIONS

13) (a) Calculate $16\frac{2}{3}\%$ of £54.
    (b) Express 80 km in miles.
    (c) A man receives £85 per week.
        (i) What is his annual salary?
        (ii) If he were paid an equal amount each calendar month, how much would he receive each month? Give the answer to the nearest penny.

14) (a) Calculate $37\frac{1}{2}\%$ of £160.
    (b) What is the price to the customer of an article priced at £160 and sold with $3\frac{3}{4}\%$ cash discount?
    (c) A man has to pay a debt of £182 in equal weekly instalments over a year. How much is the weekly instalment he has to pay?

15) Find the exact value of the following.
    (a) 325 divided by $12\frac{1}{2}$.
    (b) 1262×498.
    (c) $\dfrac{12^2 + 6^2}{3^3}$

16) (a) A motor car tank's capacity is 9 gallons of petrol. How much is this in litres, to the nearest litre? (Note: A litre is 1·76 pints.)
    (b) A motor car travels 40 miles. How many kilometres does this represent? (A kilometre is $\frac{5}{8}$ of a mile.)

17) (a) Reduce $\frac{715}{3575}$ to its lowest terms.
    (b) Find 15% of £34.
    (c) A man's annual salary is £3614. How much per week does he get?

18) (a) Add 7 km 354 m, 48 cm, 4000 mm, 71 cm, and 710 m 83 cm, giving the answer in metres.
    (b) How many litres should a tank scheduled for 9 gallons hold? (One litre = 1·76 pints.) Answer to one decimal place.
    (c) How much less than or more than three miles is 5000 metres? (8 km = 5 miles.) Answer to the nearest metre.
    d) Express 45 seconds as a fraction of a day, in its lowest terms.

19) (a) Find the circumference in centimetres of a circle of radius 140 mm.
    (b) A rectangular table, of area 5 m² is 250 cm wide. What is its length in centimetres?
    (c) A triangle has a base of 8 cm and a vertical height of 6 cm. Calculate its area.

20) (a) A paving stone measures 76 cm by 60 cm. How many are needed to cover an area 38 m by 48 m?
    (b) A rectangular room is 6 m long, 4 m wide and 2·5 m high. One quarter of the wall space is taken up by windows, doors, etc. The remainder is covered by wallpaper 50 cm wide. What length of wallpaper is required?

21) (a) A retailer's weekly takings in one month were as follows: £105·75, £96·74, £106·38, £90·95. What were his average weekly takings? What might he expect to take in one year (52 weeks) estimated from this average?
    (b) 5 men earn £80 each and 2 men earn £136 each. What were the average earnings per man?

22) The average diameter of a certain specie of tree of varying ages is shown in the table below:

Age in years	5	10	15	20	30	50
Diameter (cm)	4·5	6	8·5	12	22	54

Draw a graph of this information plotting age on the horizontal axis. From your graph find the average diameter of a tree which is 40 years old and the age at which the average diameter will be 17 cm.

23) (a) The figures below, showing the populations of seven villages, were taken at random after a census. Find the median.
    1864 2467 1392 1459 2134
    9803 5072
    (b) A Pie Chart is used to show the weekly expenditure on a motor car. If the total weekly expenditure is £12 and the angle of the sector representing Tax and Insurance is

60°, how much does 'Tax and Insurance' cost per week?

24) Find the cost of:
(a) 4 pens at 25p each.
(b) 3 metres of cloth at £1·99 per metre.
(c) 7 kg of potatoes when 3 kg cost 13½p.
(d) 29 litres of petrol at 42p per litre.
(e) A piece of glass 1 metre long and 55 cm wide, when 1 m² of glass costs £3·00.

25) (a) $\frac{3}{40}$ as a % is:

    a 3%   **b** 7½%   **c** 40%
    d 75%   **e** 97%

(b) A boy scored 70% in a test. If the maximum mark was 40, then the boy's mark was:

    a 4 **b** 10 **c** 28 **d** 30 **e** 35

(c) During a sale, a shop reduced the price of everything by 10%. What was the Sale Price of an article originally priced at £4·30?

    a £0·43 **b** £3·40 **c** £3·87
    d £3·97 **e** £4·73

26) (a) The value of $0·6 \times 0·04$ is:

    a 0·24 **b** 0·64 **c** 0·024
    d 2·4 **e** 0·0024

(b) In the number 460·23 the actual value represented by the digit 3 is:

    a 3 **b** $\frac{3}{10}$ **c** 30 **d** $\frac{3}{100}$

(c) Calculate the average of 1, 2, 5, 7 and 15.

    a 6 **b** 30 **c** 7 **d** 15 **e** 4

27) A record player costs £30 but is offered for sale at a reduction of ¼ of this price.
(a) What is the sale price? I actually pay for the record player by making a deposit of £5 followed by 6 monthly payments of £3·50.
(b) How much will the record player cost by paying for it in this way?
In the same shop records are offered for sale at a reduction of 15%.
(c) How much will I have to pay for a record which would have cost £2·50?

28) An investigation was carried out into the reasons for absence or for late arrival at a factory on a particular Monday morning. The results of the investigation were as follows:

Missed the bus	25%
Sickness	38%
Overslept	11%
Had a cold	21%
Car trouble	5%

(a) On the graph paper draw a bar chart to illustrate these statistics. Use a scale of 2 cm to represent 5% on the vertical axis.
(b) If the information had been represented on a pie chart, calculate the angle at the centre which would have been required for the sector representing 'Sickness'.
(c) If 1200 people worked at the factory and, on that particular morning, 20% were absent or arrived late, calculate how many people missed the bus.

29) On a certain brand of matches it states on the box that the average contents is 36 matches. The contents of 9 different boxes were counted with the following results.

32, 37, 35, 29, 37, 32, 40, 37, 36.

(a) What is the mode for this set of figures?
(b) What is the median number of matches in a box?
(c) Calculate the mean number of matches to a box.

30) (a) A shopkeeper wishes to price an article so that he will make a profit of 25% on his cost price after allowing a discount of 5% for cash. At what will he price an article which costs him £84?
(b) A manufacturer issues a price list of his goods. A retailer when buying from the manufacturer receives a discount of 20% off the list price. A customer buying for cash is allowed a discount of 5% by the retailer. Calculate the percentage gross profit that the retailer will make when he sells goods for cash.

Answers

ANSWERS TO CHAPTER 1

Exercise 1
1) 457   2) 9536   3) 7777   4) 3008
5) 705   6) 30 028   7) 5090   8) 4904
9) 125 906   10) 3 800 007
11) 95 827 000   12) 300 000 009
13) two hundred and twenty five
14) eight thousand three hundred and twenty one
15) three thousand and seventeen
16) three thousand nine hundred and sixty
17) one thousand eight hundred and seven
18) twenty thousand and four
19) seventeen thousand
20) one hundred and ninety eight thousand, three hundred and seventy six
21) two hundred thousand and five
22) seven million, three hundred and sixty five thousand, two hundred and thirty one
23) twenty seven million, three hundred and nine

Exercise 2
1) 351   2) 4570   3) 58 190
4) 8 579 649   5) 126 331

Exercise 3
1) 32   2) 335   3) 14   4) 1558
5) 9226

Exercise 4
1) 11   2) 32   3) 36   4) 18

Exercise 5
1) 6   2) 35   3) 54   4) 32
5) 63   6) 15   7) 81   8) 42

Exercise 6
1) 928   2) 9334   3) 1 010 829
4) 4 483 887   5) 1 022 656

Exercise 7
1) 246   2) 56   3) 433 remainder 3
4) 1842 remainder 1   5) 624 remainder 5

Exercise 8
1) 546 remainder 4   2) 1264
3) 309 remainder 1   4) 909 remainder 2
5) 903 remainder 1   6) 1701

7) 59 817   8) 5923

Exercise 9
1) 13   2) 10   3) 57   4) 7
5) 35   6) 15   7) 45   8) 74
9) 13   10) 20

Mental test 1
1) 28   2) 42   3) 350   4) 46
5) 11   6) 9   7) 62   8) 5
9) 25   10) 65   11) 84   12) 133
13) 819   14) 21   15) 103   16) 2799
17) 217   18) 143   19) 108   20) 23

Self-test 1
1) b   2) a   3) e   4) a
5)(a) 22 676   (b) 22 527   (c) 15 891
6)(a) b   (b) c   (c) a   7)(a) 1105
(b) 1316   (c) 6116   (d) 261   (e) 114
(f) 903   8)(a) 114 786
(b) 7 625 868   (c) 37 883 967
(d) 23 114 250   (e) 56 770 371
(f) 57 566 124   9)(a) 11 587
(b) 539   (c) 48   (d) 18   10)(a) 17
(b) 12   (c) 6   (d) 72   11)(a) 4
(b) 5   (c) 9   (d) 4   (e) 11
(f) 4, 8, 16   12)(a) b   (b) a   (c) b
(d) c   (e) a   13) true   14) false
15) false   16) true   17) false   18) true
19) false   20) true

ANSWERS TO CHAPTER 2

Exercise 10
1) $\frac{21}{28}$ 2) $\frac{12}{20}$ 3) $\frac{25}{30}$ 4) $\frac{7}{63}$
5) $\frac{8}{12}$ 6) $\frac{4}{24}$ 7) $\frac{24}{64}$ 8) $\frac{25}{35}$

Exercise 11
1) $\frac{1}{2}$ 2) $\frac{3}{5}$ 3) $\frac{1}{8}$ 4) $\frac{3}{5}$
5) $\frac{7}{8}$ 6) $\frac{3}{4}$ 7) $\frac{5}{7}$ 8) $\frac{18}{35}$
9) $\frac{2}{3}$ 10) $\frac{2}{3}$

Exercise 12
1) $3\frac{1}{2}$ 2) 2   3) $2\frac{1}{5}$ 4) $1\frac{1}{11}$
5) $2\frac{5}{8}$ 6) $\frac{19}{8}$ 7) $\frac{51}{10}$ 8) $\frac{26}{3}$
9) $\frac{127}{20}$ 10) $\frac{31}{7}$

Exercise 13
1) 24 2) 60 3) 12 4) 24
5) 40 6) 100 7) 160 8) 120
9) 420 10) 5040

Exercise 14
1) $\frac{1}{2}, \frac{7}{12}, \frac{2}{3}$ and $\frac{5}{6}$ 2) $\frac{3}{4}, \frac{6}{7}, \frac{7}{8}$ and $\frac{9}{10}$
3) $\frac{11}{20}, \frac{3}{5}, \frac{7}{10}$ and $\frac{13}{16}$ 4) $\frac{3}{5}, \frac{5}{8}, \frac{13}{20}$ and $\frac{3}{4}$
5) $\frac{9}{14}, \frac{11}{16}, \frac{7}{10}$ and $\frac{3}{4}$ 6) $\frac{3}{8}, \frac{2}{5}, \frac{5}{9}$ and $\frac{4}{7}$

Exercise 15
1) $\frac{5}{6}$ 2) $\frac{13}{10} = 1\frac{3}{10}$ 3) $1\frac{1}{8}$
4) $\frac{11}{20}$ 5) $2\frac{1}{8}$ 6) $1\frac{47}{120}$ 7) $4\frac{15}{16}$
8) $14\frac{4}{15}$ 9) $13\frac{23}{56}$ 10) $10\frac{2}{3}$ 11) $11\frac{5}{16}$
12) $10\frac{13}{15}$

Exercise 16
1) $\frac{1}{6}$ 2) $\frac{2}{15}$ 3) $\frac{1}{6}$ 4) $\frac{1}{2}$
5) $\frac{1}{24}$ 6) $\frac{7}{8}$ 7) $2\frac{2}{7}$ 8) $1\frac{1}{5}$
9) $2\frac{19}{40}$ 10) $\frac{51}{160}$ 11) $\frac{41}{80}$

Exercise 17
1) $1\frac{3}{8}$ 2) $\frac{7}{20}$ 3) $6\frac{7}{8}$ 4) $\frac{2}{3}$
5) $8\frac{13}{80}$ 6) $12\frac{9}{40}$ 7) $2\frac{21}{80}$ 8) $8\frac{23}{32}$
9) $3\frac{7}{8}$ 10) $3\frac{31}{100}$

Exercise 18
1) $\frac{8}{15}$ 2) $\frac{15}{28}$ 3) $\frac{10}{27}$ 4) $1\frac{19}{36}$
5) $4\frac{9}{10}$ 6) $6\frac{2}{3}$ 7) $1\frac{32}{45}$ 8) $2\frac{53}{56}$

Exercise 19
1) $1\frac{1}{3}$ 2) 4 3) $\frac{7}{16}$ 4) $1\frac{1}{2}$
5) $\frac{1}{24}$ 6) 4 7) $6\frac{3}{4}$ 8) $8\frac{1}{4}$
9) 12 10) 100 11) 3 12) 2

Exercise 20
1) $\frac{3}{5}$ 2) 8 3) $1\frac{1}{3}$ 4) $1\frac{1}{2}$
5) $\frac{2}{3}$ 6) $\frac{25}{26}$ 7) $1\frac{1}{5}$ 8) $3\frac{5}{6}$

Exercise 21
1) $3\frac{13}{14}$ 2) 5 3) $2\frac{1}{2}$ 4) $\frac{5}{6}$
5) $\frac{2}{3}$ 6) $2\frac{1}{2}$ 7) $1\frac{2}{5}$ 8) $\frac{2}{3}$
9) $\frac{1}{6}$ 10) $\frac{3}{25}$

Mental test 2
1) $\frac{5}{8}$ 2) $\frac{11}{20}$ 3) $\frac{3}{10}$ 4) $\frac{7}{8}$
5) 1 6) $\frac{7}{12}$ 7) $\frac{1}{10}$ 8) $\frac{2}{7}$
9) $\frac{3}{8}$ 10) 8 11) 12 12) $\frac{1}{8}$
13) $\frac{1}{3}$ 14) $\frac{1}{2}$ 15) $\frac{5}{6}$

Self-test 2
1) b 2) a and e 3) c 4) a
5) d 6) a 7) c and d 8) e
9) b 10) d 11) b 12) c
13) c 14) b, c 15) b 16) true
17) false 18) true 19) true 20) true
21) true 22) true 23) true 24) true
25) false

ANSWERS TO CHAPTER 3

Exercise 22
1) 0·7 2) 0·37 3) 0·589 4) 0·009
5) 0·03 6) 0·017 7) 8·06 8) 24·0209
9) 50·008 10) $\frac{2}{10}$ 11) $4\frac{6}{10}$ 12) $3\frac{58}{100}$
13) $437\frac{25}{100}$ 14) $\frac{4}{1000}$ 15) $\frac{36}{1000}$ 16) $400\frac{29}{1000}$
17) $\frac{1}{1000}$ 18) $\frac{329}{10000}$

Exercise 23
1) 3 2) 11·5 3) 24·04 4) 58·616
5) 54·852 6) 4·12 7) 15·616 8) 0·339
9) 0·812 10) 5·4109

Exercise 24
1) 41, 410, 4100 2) 24·2, 242, 2420
3) 0·46, 4·6, 46 4) 3·5, 35, 350
5) 1·486, 14·86, 148·6
6) 0·017 53, 0·1753, 1·753
7) 48·53 8) 9 9) 1700·6 10) 5639·6

Exercise 25
1) 0·36, 0·036, 0·0036
2) 6·4198, 0·641 98, 0·064 198
3) 0·007, 0·0007, 0·000 07
4) 51·04, 5·104, 0·5104
5) 0·0352, 0·003 52, 0·000 352
6) 0·054 7) 0·002 05 8) 0·004
9) 0·000 008 6 10) 0·062 742 8

Exercise 26
1) 743·0266 2) 0·951 534
3) 0·2888 4) 7·411 25
5) 0·001 376

Exercise 27
1) 1·33 2) 0·016 3) 189·74 4) 4·1066
5) 43·2

ANSWERS

Exercise 28

1) 24·8658, 24·87, 25
2) 0·008 357, 0·008 36, 0·0084
3) 4·9785, 4·98, 5   4) 22   5) 35·60
6) 28 388 000, 28 000 000
7) 4·1498, 4·150, 4·15   8) 9·20

Exercise 29

1) $200 \times 0·005 = 1$ 2) $32 \times 0·25 = 8$
3) $0·7 \times 0·1 \times 2 = 0·14$
4) $80 \div 20 = 4$ 5) $0·06 \div 0·003 = 20$
6) $30 \times 30 \times 0·03 = 27$
7) $\dfrac{0·7 \times 0·006}{0·03} = 0·14$ 8) $\dfrac{30 \times 30}{10 \times 3} = 30$

Exercise 30

1) 0·25   2) 0·75   3) 0·375   4) 0·6875
5) 0·5   6) 0·6667   7) 0·6563   8) 0·4531
9) 1·8333   10) 2·4375   11) 0·333   12) 0·778
13) 0·133   14) 0·189   15) 0·356   16) 0·232
17) 0·525   18) 0·384   19) 0·328   20) 0·567

Exercise 31

1) $\frac{1}{5}$ 2) $\frac{9}{20}$ 3) $\frac{5}{16}$ 4) $2\frac{11}{20}$
5) $\frac{3}{400}$ 6) $2\frac{1}{8}$ 7) 0·0001
8) 0·001 875

Mental test 3

1) 5   2) 1·77   3) 33·41   4) 1·22
5) 2·12   6) 0·08   7) 11·5   8) 5·81
9) 5·72   10) 0·48   11) 9·27   12) 0·12
13) 0·15   14) 2·4   15) 1·3

Self-test 3

1) b   2) b   3) d   4) a
5) c   6) d   7) c   8) d
9) c   10) a   11) true   12) false
13) true   14) false   15) false   16) false
17) true   18) true   19) true   20) true

ANSWERS TO CHAPTER 4

Exercise 32

1) 68 p, 63 p, 58½ p
2) 216 p, 359½ p, 1768 p
3) £0·35, £0·78½, £0·06, £0·03
4) £2·46, £9·83½, £265·32
5)(a) £10·06   (b) £215·58
   (c) £5·42½   (d) £2·35   (e) £2·00½
6)(a) £2·24   (b) £7·93
   (c) £68·61½   (d) £0·78   (e) £2·09½

Exercise 36

1) £1·80   2) £6·37½   3) £16·98½   4) £168·84
5) 13 p   6) 21½ p   7) £1·30½   8) £2·16½

Exercise 37

1) £67·50 + £303·75 + £477·00 + £192·00 =
    £1040·75
2) £124·00 + £31·50 + £40·80 + £12·50 =
    £208·80
3) £87·75 + £183·60 + £154·35 + £140·40 =
    £566·10
4) £53·92 + £236·50 + £237·30 + £525·00 +
    £309·00 = £1361·72
5) £19·80 + £9·00 + £61·75 + £22·44 + £13·92
    = £126·91

Mental test 4

1) £7·23   2) 60 p   3) £120   4) 7½ p
5) 1½ p   6) £3   7) 20 p   8) £4·95
9) £7·92   10) £15

Self-test 4

1) true   2) true   3) false   4) true
5) true   6) false   7) true   8) true
9) true   10) true

ANSWERS TO CHAPTER 5

Exercise 38

1)(a) 5 630   (b) 680   (c) 17 698
   (d) 5·92   (e) 0·68   (f) 6·895
   (g) 0·073   (h) 45·97   (i) 0·798
   (j) 0·005
2)(a) 9·753   (b) 0·259   (c) 0·058
   (d) 0·029 85   (e) 0·790 685
3)(a) 468   (b) 78·2   (c) 516 000   (d) 389·7
   (e) 8·8
4)(a) 1234   (b) 580 000   (c) 258
   (d) 3890   (e) 52
5)(a) 0·530   (b) 35
   (c) 0·002 473   (d) 0·597 600
   (e) 58 000   (f) 127 000
6)(a) 56   (b) 0·096   (c) 8630   (d) 81
   (e) 0·584
7)(a) (i) 0·450   (ii) 8·762
   (b) (i) 2650   (ii) 632
8) 46

Exercise 39

1) 4507   2) 1·393   3) 6·2 cm   4) 19·7675
5) 4·25 kg   6) 74 kg   7) 14·01 km
8) 42·45 m

Exercise 40

1) 39·95 m 2) 505·6 m
3) 18·98 m 4) 51 pieces; 42 cm
5) 36   6) 1 053 kg 7) 6   8) 12·6 m

Exercise 41

1) 48 m 2) 148·8 m 3) 27 m 4) 6·02 m
5) 5 rolls 6) 6 rolls 7) 6·53 m

Mental test 5

1) 15·45 m 2) 57·9 cm 3) 9 700 4) 376
5) 5·98 m 6) 1·80 m 7) 9 g 8) 14 m
9) 1 560 kg 10) 200 11) 200 kg
12) 25

Self-test 5

1) true 2) false 3) false 4) false
5) false 6) true 7) true 8) true
9) false 10) true 11) true 12) true
13) false 14) false 15) true 16) true

ANSWERS TO CHAPTER 6

Exercise 42

1)(a) 56 cm^2 (b) 220 mm^2
   (c) 630 m^2
2) 1·036 m^2 3) 1·7424 m^2
4) 28·42 m^2 5) 62 m^2 6) 174 m^2
7)(a) 53·55 m^2 (b) 37·23 m^2 (c) 16·32 m^2
8)(a) 1200 mm^2 (b) 275 mm^2
   (c) 259·5 mm^2 (d) 774 mm^2
   (e) 1050 mm^2 (f) 1094 mm^2

Exercise 43

1) 144 cm^2 2) 2400 3) 66 m^2
4) 56 cm^2 5) 0·0455 m^2
6) 4 m 7) 7·2 m 8) 23·4 cm^2

Exercise 44

1) 108 cm^2 2) 22·125 cm^2
3) 40 cm^2 4) 94·24 cm^2
5) 10 cm 6) 30·615 cm^2

Exercise 45

1) 132 cm 2) 2200 mm 3) 270·2 m
4) 19·86 cm 5) 88 cm
6) 267·1 mm 7) 26·47 m
8) 4400 mm 9) 88 m
10) 10·18 m 11) 30·16 m
12) 2 m 13) 35 cm 14) 304·3 mm

Exercise 46

1) 616 cm^2 2) 385 000
3) 24·99 m^2 4) 1386 cm^2
5) 47·55 m^2 6) 30 670 mm^2
7) 141·4 cm^2 8) 581·3 mm^2
9) 116·3 m^2 10) 289·8 m^2

Mental test 6

1) 40 cm^2 2) 6 m 3) 6 cm 4) 96 cm^2
5) 20 mm 6) 16 cm^2 7) 4 m 8) 30 cm^2
9) 44 cm 10) 88 cm 11) 154 cm^2

Self test 6

1) b and c 2) a and c 3) b and d 4) b
5) c 6) b and d 7) d 8) a
9) b and c

ANSWERS TO CHAPTER 7

Exercise 47

1)(a) 168 in (b) 324 in (c) 456 in
2)(a) 3·056 yd (b) 4·139 yd
   (c) 4400 yd (d) 49 yd
3)(a) 3·125 gal (b) 2·019 gal
   (c) 0·3625 gal
4)(a) 10·63 in (b) 120·5 in
5)(a) 13·64 ℓ (b) 3·523 ℓ
   (c) 0·1421 ℓ
6)(a) 10 304 lb (b) 929·6 lb
7)(a) 2184 kg (b) 12·38 kg
   (c) 0·3969 kg (d) 462·3 kg
8)(a) 0·1372 m (b) 1·016 m
   (c) 17·74 m
9) 23 in^2 10) 144 in^2
11) 7·844 yd^2 12) 150 in^2
13) 3·100 in^2 14) 8·044 ft^2
15) 10·21 in^2 16) 12·57 in

Mental Test 7

1) $\frac{16}{5}$ 2) $2\frac{1}{2}$ 3) 4·48
4) 4·5 5) 7 m 50 cm 6) 8
7) 1·8 8) $\frac{16}{9}$ 9) 8000
10) 224

Self-Test 7

1) c 2) e 3) b
4) a 5) e 6) a
7) b 8) b

ANSWERS

ANSWERS TO CHAPTER 8

Exercise 48

1) 362·2 2) 35·78 3) 10·47 4) 70
5) 71·9 6) 2·626 7) 1·82
8) 0·000375 9) 0·0000189
10) 76·2 11) 6·6 12) 0·020 13) 136·5
14) 28467000

ANSWERS TO CHAPTER 9

Exercise 49

1) 70 2) 55 3) 36 4) 80
5) 62 6) 25 7) 90 8) 95

Exercise 50

1) 70 2) 73 3) 68 4) 81·3
5) 92·7 6) 33·3 7) 81·9

Exercise 51

1) 0·32 2) 0·78 3) 0·06 4) 0·24
5) 0·315 6) 0·482 7) 0·025 8) 0·0125
9) 0·0395 10) 0·201

Exercise 52

1)(a) 10 (b) 24 (c) 6 (d) 2·4
 (e) 21·315 (f) 2·516
2)(a) 12·5 (b) 20 (c) 16 (d) 16·3
 (e) 45·5
3) 60%; 27 4) 115 cm 5) 88$\frac{2}{3}$ cm
6)(a) £7·20 (b) £13·20 (c) £187·50
7)(a) 2·083% are bad
 (b) 3·077% are absent
 (c) 87·76% eat lunches
8) 39 643 9) 150 kg 10) 600

Exercise 53

1) 25% 2)(a) 20% (b) 16$\frac{2}{3}$%
3)(a) 13$\frac{1}{3}$% (b) 9·95%
4) 20% 5) 33$\frac{1}{3}$% 6) 12$\frac{1}{2}$% 7) 17·65%
8) 10%

Exercise 54

1) 20% 2) 25% 3) £4·50 4) £234
5) £3·75 6) £16 7) £70 8) £6
9) £225 10) £1385

Exercise 55

1) £300 2) £62·50; 33$\frac{1}{3}$%; £187·50
3) 28·57% 4) 25% 5) £24 000
6) 53·85%; £185·50 7) 23·08%
8) 20%

Exercise 56

1)(a) £8000; £15 000 (b) 21·05%; 39·47%
 (c) 34·78%; 65·22%
2)(a) £85 (b) 17%
3) £26 200; 16·03%
4)(a) £140 (b) 20% (c) 31·82%
5)(a) £15 000 (b) £4230 (c) £10 770
 (d) 23·93% (e) 35·9%

Exercise 57

1) £12·60 2) £57 3) 36 p 4) £11·25
5) £730·05

Exercise 58

1) £168 2) £10 3) £200 4) 30%
5) £304·50 6) £182·40
7) £200 8) £2328 9) £10
10) £1871; £1368·16 11) £898·61
12) £12

Mental test 9

1) 80% 2) 0·3 3) $\frac{1}{8}$ 4) 89%
5) 24 6) 3·5 7) £3·20 8) £6
9) 25% 10) £10 11) 20% 12) £36
13) £100 14) 20% 15) 25% 16) £15 000
17) £10 000 18) £20 000
19) £1·50 20) £27

Self-test 9

1) true 2) false 3) true 4) false
5) false 6) true 7) true 8) true
9) false 10) true 11) true 12) false
13) false 14) false 15) false
16) **a, b** and **d** 17) **b** 18) **a**
19) **c** 20) **b** 21) **c** 22) **b**
23) **b** 24) **c** and **d** 25) **d**

ANSWERS TO CHAPTER 10

Exercise 59

1) 22·24 mm 2) 115 kg 3) £115·20
4) 12·2 kg 5) 77 6) £82·45
7) 14·56 8) 29·83 cm 9) 23 mm
10) £1·93 11)(a) 5 (b) 8·5 (c) 8
12) 63; 63 13) 8 14) 27·5, 26, 22

Exercise 60

2) 254 4) £1·71 5) 63, 9·5

Exercise 62

5) 40 t, 20 t, 15 t and 5 t
6)(a) 350, 510, 375, 450, 475, 285, 370
   (b) 1235
7) 35 000, 26 500, 11 000, 4000
8) 25 000 000 t, 37 500 000 t 159 500 000 t
9) Clothing £4500, Furniture £6000, Stationery £1500, Sports equipment £3000, Household goods £5000
10) 14, 6, 25

Self-test 10

1) b	2) b	3) b	4) e
5) c	6) c	7) b	8) c
9) d	10) b		

ANSWERS TO REVISION QUESTIONS

1)(a) 2 km 550 m (b) $57\frac{1}{5}$
   (c) $12 \cdot 7 \times 19 \cdot 05$ cm (d) 14 ℓ
2)(a) 4800 (b) £2·80 (c) $\frac{1}{144}$
3)(a) 0·78 (b) £75 (c) 7 (d) $\frac{11}{17}$
4)(a) 3·488 187 5 (b) 52·3
5)(a) 30·40 in (b) 780·04 mm
6)(a) £4·83 (b) £2341·65
   (c) £1379·04
7)(a) 100 ℓ (b) 128 km
9)

Gross Costs	Trade Discount	Cash Discount	Net amount payable
£1000	£200	£40	£760
200	20	0	180
800	200	12	588
250	0	25	225
£2250	£420	£77	£1753

11)(a) 786·5 (b) 132 918·5
   (c) 61 035
12)(a) £570 (b) £576
13)(a) £9 (b) 128 miles
   (c)(i) £4420 (ii) £368·33
14)(a) £60 (b) £154
   (c) £3·50
15)(a) 26 (b) 628 476
   (c) $6\frac{2}{3}$
16)(a) 41 ℓ (b) 64 km
17)(a) $\frac{1}{5}$ (b) £5·10
   (c) £69·50
18)(a) 8070·02 (b) 40·9 ℓ
   (c) 200 m more (d) $\frac{1}{1920}$
19)(a) 880 mm (b) 2000 cm
   (c) 24 cm²
20)(a) 4000 (b) 75 m
21)(a) £99·95$\frac{1}{2}$; £5197·66 (b) £96
22) 36 cm; 25 years
23)(a) 2134 (b) £2
24)(a) £1 (b) £5·97
   (c) 31½p (d) £12·18
   (e) £1·65
25)(a) b (b) c (c) c
26)(a) c (b) d (c) a
27)(a) £22·50 (b) £26
   (c) £2·12$\frac{1}{2}$
28)(b) 136·8° (c) 60
29)(a) 37 (b) 36 (c) 35
30)(a) £110·53 (b) 18·75%

Index

Accounts, simple	35	Lowest common multiple	15
Addition of decimals	25	Lowest terms of a fraction	13
of fractions	16		
of numbers	2	Mark up	75
Areas	53	Margin	76
Arithmetic mean	85	Median	86
Arithmetic signs, terms and symbols	5	Mensuration of the circle	58
Averages, statistical	85	Metric system	45
		Mixed number	14
Balancing	36	Mode	86
Bar chart	92	Multiplication	5
		of fractions	18
Calculator, electronic	66		
Cancelling	19	Net profit	78
Circle, area of	59	Numbers	1
measurement of	58	Numerator of a fraction	12
Charts	87		
Checking a multiplication	7	Operations in arithmetic	1
Checks for calculations	29	with fractions	21
Combined addition and subtraction	4		
Coordinates, rectangular	88	Parallelogram, area of	56
		Percentage profit and loss	74
Decimal currency	35	Percentages	71
places	28	Petty cash book	40
to fraction conversion	32	Pictograms	94
system	24	Pie chart	91
Denominator of a fraction	12	Product in multiplication	5
Difference	5		
Discount	79	Quotient	5
Dividend	7		
Divisibility, tests for	9	Rectangle, area of	53
Division	8	Rough checks for calculations	29
of decimals	25		
of fractions	20	Scale for graphs	88
		Sequence of arithmetic operations	9
Electronic calculator	66	Significant figures	29
		Square, area of	56
Financial statements	38	Statistics	85
Fractions	12	Subtraction of decimals	25
to decimal conversion	30	of fractions	17
to percentage conversion	71	of numbers	3
		Sum in addition	5
Graphs	87		
Gross profit	78	Tests for divisibility	9
		Top heavy fractions	14
Imperial system of units	62	Trade discount	80
Improper fractions	14	Trapezium, area of	57
Invoices	43	Triangle, area of	57
with discount	81	Types of fractions	14